SUPERNORMAL WONDERS
FROM THE PSYCHIC SCENE

* The seer who predicted JFK's assassination . . .
  the woman who foresaw her husband's death
  . . . the ~~~~~~~~~~~~~~~~ ash weeks
  befo

* The ~~~~~~~~~~~~~~~~ . . . mys-
  teriou ~~~~~~~~~~~~~~~~ nge visits
  to pa

* The unexplained powers of the Great Pyramid
  . . . healers who remove diseased organs without surgery . . . ESP discoveries in Russia.

They're just a few of the extraordinary facts from
today's amazing extrasensory world of telepathy
and spiritism gathered by Alan Landsburg—TV's
#1 investigator of the Unknown.

IN SEARCH OF STRANGE PHENOMENA
by Alan Landsburg

IN SEARCH OF STRANGE PHENOMENA
Alan Landsburg

Foreword by LEONARD NIMOY

BANTAM BOOKS
TORONTO · NEW YORK · LONDON

RLI: $\dfrac{\text{VLM 9 (VLR 8–10)}}{\text{IL 9+}}$

IN SEARCH OF STRANGE PHENOMENA
A Bantam Book / March 1977

ISBN 0–553–10855–7

Published simultaneously in the United States and Canada

Bantam Books are published by Bantam Books, Inc. Its trade-
mark consisting of the words "Bantam Books" and the por-
trayal of a bantam, is registered in the United States Patent
Office and in other countries. Marca Registrada. Bantam
Books, Inc., 666 Fifth Avenue, New York, New York 10019.

PRINTED IN THE UNITED STATES OF AMERICA

To RON BECKMAN, friend and counsellor, who suggested it might be wise to search for ancient astronauts, and to the staff of ALAN LANDS-BURG PRODUCTIONS, past and present, who have explored the world in search of the intriguing elements of strange phenomena, and finally to DEBBIE BLUM whose contribution is measure-less and whose dedication is without limit.

Author's Note

The chronicle of discovery amassed in this volume is the work of many people. More than 100 researchers, scientists and skilled filmmakers participated in the various quests. For simplicity's sake we have comingled our experiences into a single first person narrative so that we may share with you the essence and excitement of the hunt without a clutter of personal introductions. As author and chief chronicler of the work we have done, I owe an enormous debt of gratitude to those who joined me in the field to explore the world of mystery. To all of those dedicated workers committed to "In Search of . . ." I say thank you. This book is as much yours as mine.

Alan Landsburg

Contents

Foreword by Leonard Nimoy   xi

1   What Are Psychic and Other
     Strange Phenomena?   1

2   The Nature of Man: The Link
     With Strange Phenomena   9

3   Pipeline to the Beyond   14

4   ESP and its Variations   27

5   Psychic Dreams and Astral
     Projection   40

6   The Case For Reincarnation   56

7   Ghosts and How to Deal
     With Them   67

8   Kirlian Photography and Psychic
     Photography—Hoax or Fact?   82

9   Criminal-Detection Work and ESP   94

10   Psychic Surgery and Healing   105

11   The Psychic World of Plants   115

12   Pyramids and Pyramidology   122

13   Improbable Monuments and
     Archaeological Puzzles   135

14   The Bermuda Triangle   149

15   Mediums and Mediumship and
     the Strange Case of Uri Geller   166

Bibliography   191

Foreword

My first working association with the television series "In Search of . . ." was a narration session in which I was asked to read aloud the major objectives of the various categories: lost civilizations, unexplained phenomena, missing persons, magic and witchcraft, myths and monsters, and finally extraterrestrials. The roll call of subjects was mind-bending. I kept on reading the sentences appended to the list but my mind was focused on the prospect of walking the electrifying path between what is known scientific fact and what is far out science fiction.

Alan Landsburg is a much honored producer of television documentary films, and his extraordinarily talented staff of directors, writers, camermen and editors were out in the field collecting some of the most unusual images ever recorded on a television screen. What appealed to me most was the very range of subjects. On the one hand we might be searching for Amelia Earhart lost on a trans-Pacific flight in 1937, on the other for the famed Count Dracula of myth and fact. Who did build Stonehenge? Where did UFOs land? Is there really life after death? Do plants speak? The quest and the questions presented virtually an unlimited source of adventure. More than a hundred people were scattered around the world recording pieces of data, clues, evidence which fulfilled Hamlet's promise that "there are more things on earth than you have dreamed of in your philosophy."

I liked the sense of butting up against old ideas and demonstrating that new explanations were possible. In pursuit of old baffling mysteries, the programs opened new directions to pursue more illuminating answers. For all of these reasons I immersed myself in the fascinating game. It's good to know that our television series "In Search of . . ." has now become something of a byword for many viewers.

This book is a chronicle of the efforts that have gone into making the television series. It's a fascinating logbook to me, filled with the excitement of overcoming the impossible and the fulfillment of discovery. I hope you find it as intriguing as I did.

Leonard Nimoy

1

What Are Psychic and Other Strange Phenomena?

In a world where the specialist is king and science is considered the guardian of reason, anything that smacks of the extraordinary is automatically suspect. In order to deal with it we must first try to fit it into one of many categories of *known* occurrences or theories. If it does not conform to our current view of the universe, we, as the average public, have one of two avenues open to us: either we can prove satisfactorily that the phenomenon does not, after all, exist—our earlier findings having been due to error or other significant factors, or we must learn to live with the notion that there are things out there (or within us) that transcend our known laws of science.

The majority of these "special phenomena" with which this book deals are properly investigated by a new science called parapsychology. Other occurrences and experiences fall into the realms of physics and geology, and still others defy any specific classification.

Through long years of observation I have become convinced that these special phenomena do indeed exist. This book is not meant to battle with skeptics (frequently uninformed) for the verity of these phenomena, already attested to abundantly by competent observers, but to try to search for the meaning, for the operational procedures involved, and ultimately for the vistas these phenomena offer mankind in future research.

1

When I decided to look into such phenomenal occurrences, in order to be better able to judge what may be scientifically valid, and what is, at best, speculation (if not wishful dreaming), I kept coming across the name of Professor Joseph B. Rhine. It seems that scientific assessment of many of the phenomena discussed here started with his pioneering work.

Professor Rhine, formerly of Duke University, invented the word *parapsychology*. A word was needed to show the difference between phenomena that did not fit into the conventional framework of psychology and yet were real in scientific terms. "Para" is the Greek word for "beyond." Parapsychology is, therefore, beyond psychology." ESP (extrasensory perception) was an earlier word of Dr. Rhine's. Thirty years ago, these terms simply didn't exist. They are among the most outstanding contributions Professor Rhine has made to this field. Long after people have forgotten about Professor Rhine and his experiments, these terms will continue to be used. Parapsychology deals with those phenomena involving the human mind or personality that can't be explained within the framework of ordinary psychology.

Extrasensory perception is the means by which paranormal phenomena are perceived. Paranormal means beyond the normal. Today something we consider normal, or ordinary, may well have been considered completely supernatural twenty years ago. Science does not stand still: what we call real today may not be real to people in the future. Extrasensory perception may become sensory perception, or ordinary perception. The phenomena being studied by parapsychologists today are extraordinary or unusual, and so are called paranormal.

Parapsychology is still trying to be accepted generally as a *regular* science. Within the next five to ten years, perhaps, we will see it recognized fully by the educational establishment. Many advances in human thought have had difficulty gaining acceptance simply because they were different from what people had previously been taught. So it is with parapsychology: it takes issue with some of the established laws of nature, or what we *think* are the laws of nature. Full acceptance of newly discovered conditions prevailing in the universe follows as day follows night, if we are to accept the laws of parapsychology. It is the most revolutionary of all the new sciences, more revolutionary than anything of a political nature. We may change our form of government, our economical or social approach, but when we are dealing with parapsychological factors, we are changing our religious, moral, and philosophical approaches. If it can be scientifically proved that man exists beyond the grave, then a new set of values will be necessary. We will have to adjust our whole way of life to this newfound truth. I sympathize with those who cannot sufficiently expand their minds to adjust to such exciting news. Many people would rather feel "safe" and remain ignorant of new knowledge than tread paths where they would have to accept new ways of looking at life. I too have had qualms about such phenomena, because if they are true, where is my free will, where is my right as a man to make my own decisions, control my destiny? Only when certain patterns began to emerge (such as in cases of reincarnation or extraterrestrial communications) did I feel confident that the powers that govern all our lives are indeed part of an orderly system, and can somehow be trusted.

It is *not* the job of the parapsychologist to find a so-called normal, logical explanation for phenomena that we know exist. It is his job to find the truth, whatever it may be, and whatever it requires of us in the way of adjusting our thinking. Having ESP, or being psychic, is not a gift of God to a few chosen individuals. It is a *natural part of human personality*. Those who do not have any ESP are lacking it because they have either disregarded or suppressed this natural, human ability. ESP is in conflict with the *conventional* views of the limitations of time and space and of cause and effect. In a work titled *A-Causal Sychronicity*, or *The Law of Meaningful Coincidence*, Carl Jung explains the *new* laws.

Briefly, it means this. Let us assume you wake up in the morning and think of your uncle Charlie, whom you haven't seen in five years. You don't know where he is or what he's doing at the present time. An hour later the telephone rings; it is someone who asks you whether you have heard anything about your uncle Charlie lately. Then you go to your job. And on your way home there is Uncle Charlie crossing the street. This is not just coincidence, according to Professor Jung, but a *meaningful* coincidence, and he shows us that there are scientifically valid connections between your impression of your uncle Charlie on arising, the questions of your caller, and the fact that you ran into your uncle Charlie shortly thereafter. This may be "illogical," but it is also quite common.

Perhaps more difficult to comprehend and more far-reaching in its consequences is the question of time and space and how the facts, as we find them in parapsychology, defy the conventional rules.

As we all know, time is something that elapses; you can go in only one direction. We are told that anything that hasn't yet come into being cannot possibly be foreseen. We couldn't possibly see or hear or know about something that happens at a great distance from us. Yet there are many fully researched, authenticated records of witnessed cases in which people experienced things happening at a distance in time or in space, either going forward or going backward, or happening simultaneously—it doesn't seem to make the slightest difference.

These phenomena exist. Those who participate in such experiences are psychic, or they wouldn't be able to do so. You have ESP, or you are psychic, if you have had some experience, even slight, that cannot be explained by the "old-fashioned" five senses, the ordinary laws of chance, of cause and effect, or direct observation. Unless you are psychic, you cannot have such extraordinary experiences. One follows the other. The degree of your ESP ability is another matter. Even though it may be slight, the statistical material in my possession appears to show that every person has some degree of psychic ability.

Like a good reporter, I began my search by looking in the library for the books Professor Rhine had written. It was then that I discovered, to my amazement, that there were *two* Professor Rhines! Dr. Joseph B. Rhine, until recently the head of Duke University's parapsychology laboratory, can be called the father of ESP, for it was he who gave psychic research this name. Less well known, but just as important, is his wife, Dr. Louisa Rhine, a biologist, whose specialty is research into the evidence of survival of personality after bodily death, and the more complicated phenomena of the human mind.

Dr. Louisa Rhine had this to say about the relationship of mind to ESP in her work, *The Sixth Sense:*

> Just what the mind is and exactly how it operates are still deep mysteries to science. But at least some explanations can be made by assuming the existence of a still largely unrecognized mental ability, to which the term "psi" has been applied.

> Telepathy and clairvoyance, both manifestations of psi, have come to be recognized as two of the main types of extrasensory perception. Both are ways of getting information about the world. In telepathy, the information comes from other people's thoughts; in clairvoyance, it comes from events or objects. A third type of ESP, by which information comes from events that have not yet taken place—in other words, the ability to look into the future—is known as "precognition." Most psi phenomena can be accounted for by one of these three, or possibly by a combination.

> There is no way of being sure. In fact a feeling is growing among parapsychologists that there may be no fundamental difference between the processes of telepathy and clairvoyance, except for one's having a subjective origin (thoughts) and the other's an objective one (things and events).

> Whatever the exact nature of psi, it seems to be unaffected by distance, functioning just as easily whether the persons, objects, or events are separated by a room, town, continent, or ocean. And in the case of precognition, we see that psi, even more incredibly, is apparently also independent of time.

Since the facts are amply supported by the evidence, we must find a scientific edifice in which the existing conditions fit, rather than continue to try to force paranormal occurrences into the *existing* laws of science. They simply do not fit. When the facts require a reevaluation of older laws, then these laws must be revised to fit the facts; otherwise, science becomes a living lie, says Professor Hans Holzer in his book *The Truth About ESP*.

The growing interest in extrasensory perception has reached the Russians. This is a touchy matter for Communists, since the existence of a nonphysical factor in human personality—that which the churches call the soul—is inadmissible in dialectical Marxism.

However, there has always been an underground interest in psychic subjects in Russia. Despite governmental restrictions, psychic realities have been shown to exist—clandestine seances have been held, and ghosts have been seen by competent observers. But officially these subjects were forbidden, and could bring a practitioner into the chilly climate of outer Siberia. Now the Cold War is thawing, at least in science. Although I've never discussed my search for special phenomena with a Russian, the books by Ostrander and Schroeder offer ample detail of the struggle now going on behind the Iron Curtain to "fit" parapsychology into the political scene. At least the Communists are honest enough to admit that phenomena exist—something that some of our own old-line scientists won't do.

According to a June 2, 1963, report in the New York *Daily News,* something new was happening under the Muscovite sun:

The Russians are pouring money and manpower into an effort to harness something more awesome than the atom—the human mind.

Already they have: 1. Established at least eight research centers specializing in telepathic experiments —all on an academic-scientific level. The best-known one is at Leningrad University. 2. Established an exchange program with India to study psychological and mental disciplines of the yogis and their alleged capacities to transmit ideas at will. 3. Organized teams of scientists—physiologists, psychologists, physicists, zoologists, biologists, neurologists, mathematicians, cyberneticians, and electronics engineers—to investigate telepathy, find out how it works, and devise means of practical application.

The head of the Leningrad parapsychology laboratory, the late Leonid L. Vasiliev, was the author of *Mysterious Phenomena of the Human Psyche*. After a detailed, lengthy account of the nature of extrasensory perception, hypnosis, and other related states, Vasiliev paid public respect to his masters by declaring worthless all evidence of the existence of a *nonphysical* component in human personality. This was to be expected, for parapsychology cannot freely be studied in Russia. But that it exists at all is progress.

On the whole, the press has been, and still is, hostile to the very notion of ESP. Occasionally there are exceptions, when an individual editor or writer knows how to overcome editorial policies, which are usually against the subject.

However, some well-documented accounts of ESP studies have been published in some magazines and weeklies. It is interesting to note that "alternate explanations" are offered in such articles, but at least the facts are fully presented.

Even the *Wall Street Journal* devoted considerable space to ESP, and in the November 17, 1965, issue, reporter William D. Hartley presented this account:

To its many critics, parapsychology has long been linked with fumbling attempts to analyze and draw inferences from the visions of crackpots and frauds, and to explain why things go bump in the night. The researchers themselves have been attacked as charlatans and incompetents, and their experiments derided as poorly controlled. Now, however, criticism has abated somewhat, and scientists and scholars seem more willing to concede that ESP and other psychic phenomena are fitting subjects for scientific inquiry.

Study in the field remains severely restricted. J. Gaither Pratt, a parapsychologist at the University

of Virginia, estimates there are probably no more than
a dozen or so full-time, academically trained parapsychologists at work in the U.S. and perhaps fifty
other qualified researchers who labor part-time on the
specialty. He also estimates that no more than five
hundred thousand dollars a year goes into parapsychological research, pin money compared to outlays in
other fields.

Douglas Dean, principal investigator at Newark
College Psi Communications Project, believes that
successful, dynamic executives may use precognition
unconsciously in making decisions.

The highly respected Menninger Foundation is
sponsoring a project, financed by two private grants,
aimed at finding out if there is any connection between
creative ability in an individual and ESP capability.

According to Martin Ebon, well-known editor and
researcher, belief and skepticism rival each other in the
lives of many outstanding men who have recorded psychic experiences or shown unusual fascination with the
so-called occult. Experiences such as telepathic impressions or prophetic dreams seem to be part of everyday
life. Although they happen to just about everybody,
most of us do not remember them; our culture has con-
ditioned us to ignore the uncanny as unhealthy or fear-
inspiring, although it seems to permeate the civilization
of our day just as much as it did earlier cultures. Some
psychic events are unique in their dramatic impact.
They may change a man's whole outlook on life; they
may frighten him into retreat from everything that is
inexplicable; or they may arouse his curiosity toward
deeper understanding of his extrasensory capacities.

2
The Nature of Man:
The Link With Strange Phenomena

When phenomena are observed and recorded by man, his abilities as an observer and recorder must be considered when evaluating the phenomena themselves. For if man is incompetent as observer and evaluator, his conclusions cannot be accurate. But man is not incompetent—far from it. Those among us who understand the many facets of their beings use these faculties in ways that differ markedly from people not so inclined. Only recently was it suggested by the austere Parapsychology Association that the *attitude* of the investigator (i.e., his feelings) was an important factor in the results obtained! Shades of nineteenth-century materialism with its insistence that personal elements have no place in science! But of course they do; the doctor with good "bedside manners" frequently cures a patient who cannot be helped in the indifferent atmosphere of a hospital. The dedicated researcher comes up with data that the average student, who is merely working to get his papers, will not be able to touch.

The investigation of the various kinds of special phenomena around us demands a certain attitude toward the nature of man, in order to be successful; without it, the observer will see but a fraction of the existing happenings. But the acceptance of the triune nature of man (body, mind, spirit) is becoming greater and greater in scientific circles, even if the terms sometimes differ from the familiar ones.

The *progressive* idealist sees man as a duality, in

9

which a body, a physical machine, is connected and controlled by a mental force that depends on the body for its existence and continued well-being. When body dies, so does mind. By recognizing that an invisible force—the mind—could have factual reality, the progressive idealist has already traveled far from the materialistic viewpoint, but he is still distant from the full truth concerning the nature of man.

The *esoteric* thinker sees man as a whole, and acknowledges freely that mind does not dissipate when body disintegrates, but rather that mind can have an existence of its own, beyond and apart from the physical shell. Additionally, the esoteric thinker accepts the existence of a soul, or psyche, or spirit, as the *eternal* factor in human life. The psyche continues to exist not only beyond the death of body but also beyond personality, into another human form through the process of reincarnation.

The mind receives information through the nervous system, correlates it, and, through the nerve center in the brain, operates the body according to the impulses received. The psyche—sometimes considered the third layer of consciousness—makes use of both these systems, but is superior to them by virtue of greater knowledge, drawn from both internal and external sources. The external input involves a link up with the "deity force" and universal law administering it, and the internal supply of data comes from the deep recesses of the unconscious, the gateway to psychic awareness.

From the beginning of history, man has sought to understand the omnipotent power existing around him, seemingly so much greater than himself. What man fails to understand, he worships; that is, he worships that which he cannot grasp intellectually.

Religious experiences are expressed in the process of worshiping a power greater than oneself, no matter what its nature might be. In religious expression, something has to pass from physical man to the nonphysical deity concept.

In *The Human Dynamo,* Dr. Hans Holzer states:

Is man the sudden product of a willful Creator whose images we see, albeit imperfectly reflected, in the human species? Was he put on this planet earth by a *fiat,* a sudden decision, *a personal act of an intelligence greater than man?* If God, as an intelligent superpower, was out there somewhere in space, creating man, then surely He in His infinite wisdom would have wanted us to be sure of this fact. *But we are not;* some of us accept it on blind faith as a tenet of their particular religious denomination, while others reject the notion as unscientific and illogical.

But if a personal deity did not create man by one fell swoop, surely a *great law* operating in the universe around us, of which we are part, must have been governing man's appearance on this planet. Such a law must surely be the work of a power greater than ourselves, even if we are also part of this power.

The ultimate cannot be answered by man for himself unless his mind is also capable of grasping it. Therein lies the difficulty: *The part cannot be greater than the total.*

Even the Russians now acknowledge man's intra-material nature. Sheila Ostrander and Lynn Schroeder in *Psychic Discoveries Behind the Iron Curtain,* speak of "an energy body, a second body, a subtle, sensitive body that reacts almost immediately to a shift of thought or mood, or to changes in the environment."

This is a brand-new idea in Soviet biology. It's so new that the shock waves haven't been felt in other areas of science. But the aura and so-called astral body have long been dumped in the province of the parapsychologists and they were quick on the uptake. This discovery of an energy circulating in the body, neither blood nor electrical, is extremely important for parapsychology, reputable scientists told us. It might provide the long-awaited clues needed for a sensible explanation of a host of supernormal happenings from dousing to telepathy to psychic healing.

Psychic researchers who are open-minded do not doubt the existence of another dimension, into which everyone passes at the time of physical death. This nonphysical world probably is not the hereafter of religion, for there does not seem to be any evidence of the existence of a literal heaven or hell. But evidential material from reliable sources supports the theory of this secondary dimension all around us, and a large volume of experimental data has been accumulated by research groups. Many cases of paranormal experience investigated by reputable researchers can be explained by extrasensory abilities on the part of the people who had the experiences. This in itself is in opposition to orthodox scientific thinking, but it does not prove the existence of dimension beyond the physical one. However, there remains a very large body of material that can be explained only by the factual existence of another world, in which human beings continue to function emotionally and rationally, very much as they did on the earthly plane. There are so many reports of apparitions and other forms of visual communications that they simply cannot be explained away. Photographic material taken under test conditions supports the theory of a nonphysical world, in the sense that we are in the midst of it at all times, and merely exchange one density for another as we pass from the physical into the nonphysical (or spiritual) world.

I have looked with amazement at the collection of Kirlian photographs taken under test conditions at UCLA, where Dr. Thelma Moss is in charge of parapsychological experiments. In this process, electrical charges enhance living beings in order to be photographed, thus disclosing the so-called aura all living beings possess. Even more upsetting, I thought, were the psychic photographs first published in England at the turn of the century (and republished by E. W. Warrick in his memorable work, *Experiments in the Psychic*). I also saw Professor Hans Holzer deliver a lecture illustrated by slides on the subject of psychic photography, which he investigates in his book *Psychic Photography: Threshold of a New Science?* I am satisfied that none of these amazing photographs was faked or tampered with, due to the conditions under which they were obtained, either spontaneously or in experimental fashion. To me, this means that there is in fact a dimension of life beyond the earthly one, capable of some very tangible verification!

Over the years, parapsychology has shown that the nonphysical element in man is indeed reality and not merely wishful thinking or an illusion. "We can safely conclude," Dr. J. B. Rhine states, "that there is something operative in man that transcends physical law and, therefore, by definition, represents spiritual law. The universe, then, is one about which it is possible to be religious."

When Professor Rhine attempted to measure what he called the psi force in man, critics were quick to point out the dangers of a system that relied so heavily on statistics and conditions considered contrived and artificial. Since that time, however, new observations and data in nature itself have added considerable evidence to support the existence of paranormal experience. All sorts of things that seem to defy conventional scientific concepts continue to occur with regularity and have lately resulted in a good deal of rethinking on the part of the scientific community.

In the 1930s, Charles Fort collected and published data that were patently in contravention of orthodox scientific views. His followers, organized in the Fortean Society, keep adding material to the files to this day. What it all amounts to is this: either the explanations of these "unexplained" (or special) phenomena will continue to come from nonscientific sources (such as "believers" and other cultists) and a few defiant progressive scientists—or the majority of the scientific establishment will have to swallow its pride, come down from Mount Olympus, and have another good look at the growing body of evidence.

The exact definition of these special phenomena may shift with the passage of time inasmuch as new areas of science are explored; what may be special one day may be ordinary the next. But the phenomena, whatever their explanation, can no longer be explained *away*.

3
Pipeline to the Beyond

Many of those who accept spiritual concepts of life after death do so with virtually no skepticism, and believe from a personal, emotional point of view. They only replace a formal religion with an informal one; they replace an outmoded dogma, not supported by the facts as they know them, with a seemingly sensible system having a flexibility to which they can relate enthusiastically.

What is death, then? *Death* is when all bodily functions cease, and it reverses the order of things that happened at birth. Now the two major parts of man are separated again and go off in different directions: the body, deprived of its operating force, is no more than a shell and is subject to ordinary laws that affect matter. Under the influence of the atmosphere, it will rapidly decompose and is therefore quickly disposed of in all cultures, to return to the earth in various forms and contribute its basic chemicals to the soil or water.

I looked into some recent controversies concerning the moment of "legal" death: Does it occur when the vital functions cease, when the patient lapses into a coma though still "alive" (although the "soul" may already have escaped the dying body), or does it come only when the respirator or heart stimulator is finally turned off, having become useless? And what about the other, the "inner," component?

The other component—call it soul or spirit or whatever—either does not exist at all (as believed by ma-

terialists and agnostics) or it escapes bodily confine-
ment and enters "another" world. If the point of view
is that of certain formal religions, the soul lives on in
heaven or hell (after passing through an intermediary
purification process called purgatory) and can expect
what it deserves, depending on its actions while still
in the body. But if the point of view is an enlightened
scientific one, questing perhaps for hard evidence of
survival after bodily death, the soul escapes into a
dimension beyond the physical one, a dimension not
necessarily subject to moral evaluations and judgments.

Enough evidential material is on hand to show that
a force does leave the body at the time of death, and it
has even been photographed on rare occasions with
animals and plants, and observed (though not yet photographed) with human beings.

The desire to communicate with the dead is as old as
man himself. As soon as primitive man realized that
death could separate him from a loved one and that he
could not prevent that person's departure, he tried to
find a way to communicate with the dead person. But
early man did not understand nature. Death became a
person with great and sinister powers who ruled a
kingdom of darkness, somewhere far away. To communicate with a departed loved one, one would have
to have Death's permission or would have to outsmart
him. Getting Death's permission to see a loved one was
rare. The mythology of even the much more sophisticated Greeks makes a strong point of this, in the story
of Orpheus and Eurydice.

It was hard to outsmart Death. Everyman never
succeeded, nor did the wealthy Persian merchant who
ran away to Samara only to find Death waiting for him
there. In these examples Death was of course waiting
for the man himself, and it was not a question of getting
past him into his kingdom to see the departed one.

Let us assume for a moment that the dead do exist,
that they live on in a world beyond our physical world.
It would then be of the greatest interest to learn all
about the nature of that other world and the laws that
govern it. It would be important also to come to a bet-

ter understanding of the nature of this transition called death, to understand the "art of dying" as the medieval esoterics called it.

Having postulated that a nonphysical world populated by the dead does exist, we next examine the contacts between the two worlds. We find there are two kinds of communication between them: those initiated by the living, and those initiated by the dead. There is, it would appear, two-way traffic between the two worlds. Observation of so-called spontaneous phenomena that have occurred unexpectedly to actual people are just as important as induced experiments or attempts at contact. In all this we must keep an eye open for misinterpretation, deceit, or self-delusion.

It seems farfetched, however, to take for granted that thousands of people in all sorts of circumstances and under varying conditions hallucinate communications with the dead. It is more logical to assume that an extraordinary ESP experience does indeed occur to these people, even if this is contrary to orthodox scientific belief at the time. Remember, many situations now taken for granted were contrary to scientific belief at one time. Photography, airplanes, television, radio, and many other technical advances fall under that category. It is not true that science is at the peak of knowledge today, with little, if anything, startling yet to come. Science as I define it is merely a method of learning as much as possible about a given subject. It includes the qualification that one must change one's conclusions and views whenever new findings alter earlier findings. Science is therefore a continually moving force, which should be flexible and open-minded. It should welcome anyone with new ideas and should investigate those new ideas. But it rarely does. Therein lies one of man's most curious paradoxes: he wants to know desperately, but at the same time he fears any knowledge that might upset previously held beliefs. Why does a dead person want his family or friends to know that death is not the end, and that he or she is in fact very much alive in another dimension? There are two strong and compelling reasons: one is the continuing ego-consciousness of the

dead person. He wants to let those closest to him know
that he continues to exist as an entity and consequently that he wishes to be considered a continuing factor
in their lives. This is for his own sake. The second reason for this need to let the living know that life after
death exists is for *their* sake. They too will eventually
die. Why not give them the benefit of the dead person's experience? Why not do them the favor of letting
them in on the world's greatest and most important
secret: that man does not end at the grave?

Professor Hans Holzer reports:

My own encounter with this type of communication
first came in the late 50s, when I happened to drop in
at a meeting of the New York branch of the Cayce
Foundation. This foundation is also known as the
Association for Research and Enlightenment, and is
dedicated to various forms of psychic and allied research.

I sat quietly in the last row of the darkened room,
in which there were a hundred or so people listening
to a speaker. The lady was just ending her lecture-
demonstration. The lights went on, and I was sorry
to have come so late, but before I could leave, I
noticed that the speaker was making her way through
the crowd toward me. "Are you Hans Holzer?" she
asked. I nodded, thinking that someone had pointed
me out to her. Nobody had, for in those days I was
quite unknown. None of my books had yet appeared
in this field. Quickly suppressing my ego and realizing that she could not possibly have known my name, I
asked what she wanted to tell me. "I'm Betty Ritter,"
she explained, "the medium. I have a message for you
from an uncle." Well, I thought, bemused, I've got a
lot of uncles. She must have felt my skepticism, for
she added, "His initials are O.S., he's got a wife
named Alice, and she's a blond." Now I had an uncle
whose name was Otto Stransky: and he had died
tragically in a streetcar mishap in 1932, and though I
had always respected him, I hardly knew him and had
not thought of him in many years. His widow's name
was Alice. At the time of his passing she was indeed a
blond, but had long since turned gray. There was no
further message: this was it. He merely wanted me

to know he *existed.* No alternate explanation would make sense. I had not been thinking of him, and if I had I would certainly not refer to my aunt Alice as a blond, knowing full well that she had been gray for many years. Only in my uncle's memory would she still be a blond!

Rosemary Brown is an English lady who claims to be the continuing channel of expression for some of the recent past's greatest composers. The evidence is substantial and worthy of further study. Stewart Robb, the investigator of the Brown case, is not only a qualified psychic researcher but an expert musicologist. This combination of talents makes him a particularly qualified man in this instance. Why Brahms, Liszt, and others should choose a middle-class English housewife to continue writing their music for them is not as much a puzzle as one might think at first. Rosemary Brown's lack of musical training would render her a more convincing medium, perhaps. Conversely, the music of great composers such as Beethoven is openly available and the mere fact that an untutored person can write in their style is not sufficiently convincing. What is lacking, perhaps, are the intimate personal details of the composers' lives, transmitted by them to Rosemary Brown and checked out independently. If some of these personal data were unpublished but could subsequently be corroborated by a researcher through letters or other existing but inaccessible documents, we would then have a near-foolproof case for the contact between the composers and Rosemary Brown. Until this happens, the case remains open, at least to my mind.

A particularly impressive case of after-death communication was experienced in Pennsylvania. Sandra R. lives with her family in a small town southwest of Pittsburgh. Her brother, Neal, twenty-two, had been working as a bank teller for three years. Neal often said that he had a feeling that if he went into the Army he'd be killed. Consequently, his mother and sister, to whom Neal was quite close, persuaded him to join the National Guard for a six-month tour of duty. Since he was of age and would probably be drafted, he might thus

shorten his length of service. Neal finally agreed that
this was the best thing to do under the circumstances.
He quit his position at the bank, joined the National
Guard, and tried to make the best of the situation. In
April 1963 he got his orders to report to basic training
a week from the following Monday. Several times during those last days at home, he mentioned the fact that
he was to leave at 5:00 A.M. Sunday, as if this was
something important and final. On the Monday preceding his departure, he visited friends to say goodbye.
When he left home, he had the usual kiss on the cheek
for his mother, and he gaily said, "I'll see you," and
went out. He never returned. Early the following morning, the family was notified that he had been found dead
in his parked car on a lonely country road about two
miles away from his home. He had committed suicide
by inhaling carbon monoxide. The family was
shocked. At first they could not believe the news, for
they were sure he would leave some sort of note for
them. But nothing was ever found, even though they
searched the house from top to bottom. All of Neal's affairs were in order. He had left no debts or commitments, but also no message of any kind for anyone. He
was buried in his home town, and the family tried to
adjust to their great loss. His sister, Sandra, was three
years younger, but the two had been close enough to
have had many telepathic experiences in which they
would read each other's thoughts. She could not understand why her brother had not confided in her before
taking his life.

In the house, both Sandra's room and Neal's were upstairs. After the young man's death, Sandra could not
think of sleeping so near to her late brother's room, so
she slept on the roll-out divan in the living room. Friday was the day of the funeral, and it seemed to Sandra that it would never pass. Finally, after a restless,
almost sleepless night, Saturday dawned. All day long
she felt uneasy, and there was an atmospheric tension
in the air that she found almost unbearable. When night
came, Sandra asked that her mother share the couch
with her. Neither woman had taken any tranquilizers or
sleeping pills. Again they discussed the suicide from

all angles, and again failed to arrive at any conclusions. Finally, they fell asleep.

Suddenly Sandra was awakened from deep sleep by a clicking sound. It sounded exactly as if someone had snapped his fingers above her head. As Sandra became fully awake, she heard her mother stir next to her.

"Did you hear that?" her mother asked. She had also heard the strange snapping sound. Both women were now fully awake.

They both felt a tingling sensation from head to toe, as if they were plugged into an electrical socket! Some sort of current was running through them, and they were quite unable to move even a limb.

The living room was situated in the front part of the house. All the window blinds were closed, and there was no light shining through them. The only light in the room came from a doorway behind them, a doorway that led into the hall. Suddenly they noticed a light to their left. It had the brightness of an electric bulb when they first saw it. It appeared about two feet from the couch on the mother's side and was getting brighter and brighter as it moved closer to them. "What is it?" they called to each other, and then Sandra noticed that the light had a form. There was a head and shoulders encased in the light!

They were terrified. Suddenly Sandra heard herself cry out: "It's Neal!" At the moment she called out her late brother's name, the light blew up to its brightest glare. With that, a feeling of great peace and relief came over the two women.

Mrs. R., still unable to move her body, asked, "What do you want? Why did you do it?"

Then she started to cry. At that moment, waves of light in the form of fingers appeared inside the bright light, as if someone was waving goodbye. Then the light gradually dimmed, until it vanished completely.

At that instant, a rush of cold air moved across the room. A moment later they clearly heard someone walking up the stairs. They were alone in the house, so they knew it could not be a flesh-and-blood person. When the footsteps reached the top stair, it squeaked as it always had when Sandra's brother walked up the stairs. Over the years, Sandra had heard this noise time and again. There wasn't a sound in the house, except those footsteps upstairs. The two women were lying quite still on the couch, unable to move even if they had wanted to. The steps continued through the hallway, and then went into Neal's room, which was directly over the living room. Next they heard the sound of someone sitting down on the bed, and they clearly made out the noise of bedsprings giving from the weight of a person! Since the bed was almost directly over their heads down in the living room, there was no mistaking these sounds. At this moment their bodies suddenly returned to normal. The tension was broken and Sandra jumped up, turned on the light, and looked at the clock next to the couch. The time was five o'clock Sunday morning—*the exact moment* Neal had been scheduled to leave, had he not committed suicide!

With this, all was quiet again in the house. But Sandra and her mother no longer grieved for Neal. They accepted the inevitable, and began to realize that life did indeed continue in another dimension. The bond between Neal and themselves was reestablished and they felt a certain relief to know he was all right, wherever he was.

At different times since that initial goodbye visit, Mrs. R. and Sandra smelled in the house the strong aroma of Neal's favorite aftershave lotion. At the time of his death, he had a bottle of it in the glove compartment of his car. No one else in the house used aftershave lotion.

Neither Mrs. R. nor her daughter is given to hysterics. They accepted these events as perfectly natural, always carefully making sure that no ordinary explanation would fit. But when all was said and done, they knew that Neal had not let them down, after all. The bond was still unbroken.

Seemingly, the dead wish to be recognized as the people they were and are. Most of them appear looking as they did in physical life, i.e., wearing the clothes they had on when they died, or the clothes they liked to wear ordinarily. But there are also cases where the dead reportedly appeared in a simple white robe instead of their usual clothing. Perhaps the white robe is

the "ordinary" dress "over there," with the earth-type
clothing optional when and if needed. Possibly this
white robe is behind some of the legends of angels
appearing to mortals, and also of ghosts often described as being white. Ectoplasm, the material of which
apparitions of the dead are created, is white. Ectoplasm, an albumen substance that has been analyzed
in laboratories, is drawn from the bodies of the living
during seances.

It seems hard to understand why, with all the compelling evidence of cases such as Neal's, which can be
found in many works on psychic subjects, the vast
majority of the public still considers the question of
spirit survival an iffy one. Yet almost every family in
the United States has at least one event of this kind to
report—whether it is a visitation of a dead relative, a
prophetic dream, or a warning from someone "over
there" concerned with helping a living member of the
family.

Sometimes the dead wish to let someone living know
that they are across the Veil, and not merely somewhere
on earth but out of touch. Especially in the United
States, where people can move about the country freely,
without governmental requirements for registration, individuals can easily drop out of sight and may be hard
to track down. A recent case involves a young lady who
moved in with her married sister in a coastal town in
Virginia.

Mrs. S. is married to an Army man, and consequently they move around a lot. But at that time she had a
house; her sister was always welcome there. The sister
had kept company with a young man for several years
and was now engaged to him. Her weakness was cigarettes, and her young fiancé frowned on her excessive
smoking.

"I'll be back in one month to take you with me,"
he had promised before he left. "If you cut down on
cigarettes to ten a day, I'll marry you!"

Soon after he had left, strange occurrences began to
puzzle the two women. Without any reason, the sister's
clothes would be moved around in her closet. Although

neither of them had put them there, cigarette butts would be found all over the house like markers. One of her dresses disappeared completely, only to show up a week later, neatly folded, in another drawer. There were sounds of someone walking upstairs at times when there was no one in that part of the house. One day a shoe of the sister's walked down the stairs by itself—as if someone were moving it!

Mrs. S.'s husband was disturbed by the unaccountable events, and decided that they would look for another house. When he had some leave coming to him in November 1966, they decided to move back to their home town in Pennsylvania. There they found out something they had not known before: the sister's fiancé had been killed in a car accident several weeks before. As he didn't have any family, and his body had been difficult to identify, nobody had let them know of his death.

"It must have been he," Mrs. S. remarked, "trying to keep his word. After all, he did promise to get my sister in a month." Since then, nothing unusual has happened in the S. household.

If a person dies suddenly and is unable to move on, but remains in the earth's atmosphere and becomes a so-called ghost, then that person may also take with him all his unresolved problems. The problems may be major, like providing for his family or helping the young, unfinished business or lack of a legal will, or such minor matters as leaving the house of a loved one with unkind words.

Generally, a compulsion to set matters straight is what makes it necessary to communicate with living people. Once this contact has been made and the problem is understood by the living, the need of the deceased to reappear is no longer there, unless the living fails to act on the deceased communicator's request. In that case, he will probably return again and again, until he gets his way.

Delaware Avenue, one of the better residential areas in Buffalo, New York, is the home of the N. family. They share the house with its owner, Mr. N.'s uncle by marriage. After Mr. N.'s aunt died, strange knockings began to disturb the inhabitants of the house. There was never any rational explanation for these raps. Several months later, Mr. N. was cleaning out a closet in what had been the aunt's storeroom. Among the personal souvenirs and other belongings he found was a wrapped package. He picked it up, and as he did so he distinctly heard a voice—a human voice—talking to him, although he knew he was quite alone in the room. The voice was not clear enough for him to make out the words; this was late at night, and there was no radio or television on.

Mr. N. took the package with him and walked down the long hall to the bedroom where he found Mrs. N. reading in bed. For a distance of seventy-five feet, all along the way, the "voice" kept talking to him!

As he entered the bedroom, his wife looked up from her book and said: "Who was that talking to you?"

Mr. N. became very agitated, and *somehow* found himself taking the strange package to the basement. As if he had been led there, he then opened the furnace and threw the package into it. He had the strong feeling that his aunt did not wish to have that package opened or even found. As soon as the flames had destroyed the contents of the package, Mr. N.'s mood returned to normal. There were no further strange occurrences in the house after that. Evidently the aunt did not want the contents of her private package made public, and once that possibility had been prevented, her need to communicate ended.

Bernard M. is a largely self-taught scholar who lives in southern California. His literary critiques and philosophical essays have appeared in such scholarly publications as *Books Abroad*. A disability pension augments his income from writing. His mother, Frances M., was a gifted musician who had always shown an interest in psychic research. When Mr. M., Sr., who had been with the San Francisco Symphony Orchestra, passed on in 1920, the family went through difficult times, and young Bernard had to work hard to keep food on the family's table. At the age of forty-two, Mrs. M. died of a stroke while working at the Conservatory of Music and Drama in Point Loma, California.

The date of her passing was June 24, 1923, and Bernard attended the funeral a few days later. At that time, he was told that his mother's ashes would be placed in a niche in a nearby cemetery. With that reassurance, he left town for a business trip. When he returned a month later to Point Loma, he had a strange dream. His late mother appeared to him in what seemed to be a small room, quite dark, and she seemed in great distress.

"Everything went wrong," she complained. "Even my ashes are mislaid!"

Bernard, in his dream, assured her that this could not be the case. But in reply she "showed" him a little table on which was a wire basket containing a small copper box.

When he awoke the next morning, Bernard rejected what he thought was an absurd dream, brought on, no doubt, by his grief over the death of his beloved mother. But it so happened that he had previously planned to go into town to see if his mother's name had been properly inscribed on the door to the niche at the cemetery.

On the way he ran into a friend, a Mrs. L., a singer, who informed him that she had just been to the cemetery to pay her respects to Mrs. M.—and his mother's ashes were not there!

On hearing this, Bernard asked Mrs. L. to return to the cemetery with him to make inquiry. Sure enough, his father's ashes were there, but his mother's were not. He questioned the caretaker, who checked the entries in his books. "No record of a Mrs. M.," the caretaker informed him.

With mounting grief and anger, Bernard went to the funeral parlor.

After some embarrassing investigations, it was discovered that the box of ashes had never left the building. Bernard then took them personally to the niche in the cemetery, to make sure everything would be as it should.

Life in the World Unseen, by Anthony Borgia, caused a sensation; it was fiction to some, but to others it represented the first rational description of life in the spirit world. A second volume, *More About Life in the World Unseen,* was equally challenging.

According to Mr. Borgia, as death approaches, relatives or friends who have gone on before, gather around the dying person to assist in the transition from the physical to the nonphysical state. Frequently, the dying can see them already, for at the time of imminent death, the bonds between unconscious and conscious are very loose. Some valuable studies of bedside observations of the dying in various hospitals have been done by Dr. Karlis Osis of the American Society for Psychic Research. In these reports, there is frequent mention of the alleged presence in the hospital room of a long-dead relative or friend whom only the dying person can hear or see. In the past, such phenomena were brushed aside as "hallucinations of the dying," implying that *all* patients in their terminal stage are mentally incompetent, and therefore their testimony is not to be taken seriously. Today, some psychic researchers are taking a second look at this material.

4
ESP and its Variations

The definition of "extra sense" is simple enough. We speak of *extrasensory* perception when knowledge of events or facts is gained without the use of the five normal senses—touch, smell, taste, hearing, sight—or when knowledge is obtained in apparent disregard of the limitations of space and time.

It is absolutely essential, of course, that the person experiencing the sixth-sense phenomenon has no access to the knowledge, either conscious or unconscious, of the facts or events, and that his impressions are subsequently corroborated by witnesses or otherwise proved correct by the usual methods of exact science.

People have been wondering if there is such a thing as extrasensory perception ever since Dr. Joseph B. Rhine coined the term ESP. The three letters have since become fairly well known even among laymen, considered roughly the equivalent of the term "sixth sense" or having psychic abilities. ESP stands for extrasensory perception and refers to the ability of a person to perceive beyond the limits of the ordinary five senses as we know them.

A few years ago, Professor Holzer added the letters PSE to the nomenclature of parapsychology. They stand for psycho-ecstasy, a process in which a psychic person can "bring up" energy forces from his solar plexus to his brain, and thus utilize them for various purposes, such as better health, communication, extension of abilities, etc.

27

There is no such thing as a sixth sense, actually, operating separately from the ordinary five senses. There are, however, instances in which the so-called ordinary five senses do not suffice to explain certain phenomena in the mind of a subject or between two or more subjects. What we have come to call ESP, then, is not a separate sense at all, but an extension of the ordinary five senses beyond what we used to consider their limitations. I feel that, if anything, man has *five* extra senses, which are merely different expressions of the sensory apparatus and thus not separate expressions at all but parts of one's overall faculty. Under those circumstances, the ESP factor is merely an extension into another band of that one and only human faculty, and not a mysterious outside force open only to a small number of "special" people. Extrasensory perception is a *natural faculty*.

ESP is part of science. Some scientists in other areas may have doubts about its validity or its potential, just as scientists in one area frequently doubt scientists in other areas. After all, beliefs among medical doctors differ greatly, and some chemists doubt what some medical men say about the efficiency of certain drugs.

More and more, scientists wonder about the existence of one, multifaceted central force in the universe, which may in the past have been mistaken for several separate forces. Professor Albert Einstein hinted at this in his unified field theory. In the same vein, it may turn out that the various forms of unusual abilities that are responsible for many of the special phenomena reported and discussed here, are in reality only different aspects of the same complex underlying force, and that we are perhaps close to a breakthrough where we can actually manipulate this force to our benefit.

According to Evelyn de Wolfe, *Los Angeles Times* staff writer, "The phenomenon of ESP remains inconclusive, ephemeral and mystifying, but for the first time in the realm of science, no one is ashamed to say they believe there is such a thing."

The technical/economic magazine *Nation's Business* of April 1971, states: "Dollars May Flow from the Sixth Sense. Is there a link between business success and extrasensory perception? We think the role of precognition deserves special consideration in sales forecasting. Wittingly or unwittingly, it is probably already used there. Much more research needs to be done on the presence and use of precognition among executives, but the evidence we have obtained indicates that such research will be well worthwhile."

The Russians delved fully into the subject of ESP phenomena. They went into the field wholesale: at this time there are at least eight major universities in the Soviet Union with full-time, fully staffed research centers in parapsychology. What is more, there are no restrictions placed upon those working in this field, and they are free to publish anything they like, whether or not it conforms to dialectical Marxism. In the United States, bickering between those who accept and those who categorically reject the reality of ESP phenomena still hampers funding.

Mat Freedland, reviewing the book *Psychic Discoveries Behind the Iron Curtain* for the *Los Angeles Times,* said:

> Scientists in Eastern Europe have been succeeding with astonishingly far-reaching parapsychology experiments for years. The scope of what Communist countries like Russia, Czechoslovakia, and even little Bulgaria have accomplished in controlled scientific psi experiments makes the western brand of ESP look namby-pamby indeed. Instead of piddling around endlessly with decks of cards and dice like Dr. J. B. Rhine of Duke University, Soviet scientists put one telepathically talented experimenter in Moscow and another in Siberia, 1200 miles away.

People accept theories, beliefs, or philosophies largely on the basis of who supports them, not necessarily on the facts alone; they are likely to follow a highly regarded person who supports a new belief. So it was something of a shock to learn, several years after his passing, that Franklin Delano Roosevelt had frequently attended seances in which his late mother, Sara Delano, appeared to him and gave him advice in matters of state. King George V of England attended seances also. Even today, the English royal family is partial to psychical research, although very little of it is published. Less secret is the case of Canada's late prime minister William Mackenzie King, who was a spiritualist.

Interestingly, we find that the number of people who accept the existence of ESP is much larger than that of those who believe in spirit survival or the more advanced forms of occult beliefs. To the average mind, at least, belief in spirit survival, ghosts, reincarnation, etc., seems to require more commitments than the purely scientific. There is a very basic difference between ESP and the more advanced forms of the occult: with ESP, one need not necessarily accept survival of human personality beyond bodily death.

Jeane Dixon states:

> Writers often set out to debunk me and the whole field of ESP, and they search only for the evidence that will bolster their argument. I remember when Jess Stern came to see me and had dinner with me, he was going to debunk everything about ESP, and me along with it. And when I was able to tell him things he knew I had no normal way of knowing, and when he interviewed people who knew me and also saw me on NBC accurately predicting Sputnik would be orbited —then he knew there was something to it.

Knowledge of what lies ahead matters most, since it allows the possibility of preparing for future events in one way or another. Knowledge of contemporary events, even the space shots, is less dramatic. It is true that Swedenborg told his audience of the Great Fire of Stockholm while hundreds of miles away and while the fire was actually going on. The effect was dramatic, but his audience also realized that there was little they could do about the event itself and it would take some time before the truth of Swedenborg's statements could be confirmed. As it turned out, his vision was entirely correct.

The majority of *precognitive* experiences occur spontaneously and unsought. Precognition is the ability to foretell, to have accurate information about events, situations, and people before the time that we

become consciously aware of them. Some people may
have a hint that a precognitive situation is about to occur: they may feel odd, experience giddiness or a sensation of tingling in various parts of the body, or simply have a vague foreboding that a psychic experience
is about to take place. To other people, these things
come out of left field, taking them completely by surprise. Many find that the ability to foretell the future
is more of a burden than a blessing, because they begin
to believe that foretelling bad events may in some way
cause them. Of course this is not true. By tuning in to
the existing conditions and, through ESP, picking up
that which lies ahead, the receiver is acting merely as
a channel, without responsibility for the event itself, its
timing, the results of the event, or the moral implications of it. The receiver has no more control over what
he foretells than a radio set has control over programs
coming through it.

But long before Jeane Dixon came into the lime-
light, she startled Washington friends with uncanny predictions that, often unfortunately, came true. On the
morning after the assassination of President Kennedy,
the New York *Journal-American* carried a brief account
of Mrs. Dixon's role in the great tragedy:

> The tragic death of President John F. Kennedy was
> forecast in 1956 and reiterated twice in the past week
> by Jeane Dixon, a Washington, D.C., socialite and
> seer.
>
> For years she has electrified Capitol Hill with a suc-
> cession of eerie and accurate predictions of things to
> come.
>
> "As for the 1960 election, it will be dominated by
> labor and won by a Democrat. But he will be assassi-
> nated or die in office, not necessarily in his first term."

In 1934 Thomas Menes, a Spanish seer known for
his frequently accurate prophecies, announced that
Chancellor Dollfuss of Austria would die violently
within three months. The date was May 23.

During the summer, when the Nazis tried to seize
power in Austria, a group of them came upon Dollfuss

in a cabinet meeting and assassinated him. This was on July 25, only two months and two days after the Madrid prophet's prediction was made. Thomas Menes became famous overnight.

Professor Hans Holzer reported a particularly evidential case of precognition experienced by a Miss Lauterer of New York, who gave the following account:

One night not long ago in New York, as I was in bed, halfway between sleep and being fully awake, I saw a face as clearly as one sees a picture projected on a screen. I saw it with the mind's eye, for my eyes were closed. This was the first experience that I can recall, where I saw, in my mind, a face I had never seen before.

About six weeks later, I received an invitation to go to Colombia, South America; I stayed on a banana plantation in Turbo, which is a primitive little town in the Gulf of Aruba. Most of the people who live there are the descendants of runaway slaves and Indian tribes. Transportation is by launch or canoe from the mainland to the tiny cluster of nearby islands. The plantation was located near the airport on the mainland, as was the Customs Office. The village of Turbo is on an island or peninsula.

One Sunday afternoon I went into town with my host, an American, and my Colombian friend. As we walked through the dirty streets bordered with sewerage drains, and looked around at the tin-roofed hovels and the populace of the place, I thought: this is the edge of the world.

Sunday seemed to be the market day; the streets were crowded with people mostly of two hues, black and red-skinned. As we passed a drug store, walking single file, a tall, handsome, well-dressed young man caught my attention. He seemed as out of place as I and my companions did. He did not look at me, even as I passed directly in front of him. It struck me as strange. South American men always look at women in the most frank manner.

Also, he looked familiar, and I realized that this was the face I had seen in my mind, weeks before in New York!

The following day we were invited to cocktails by our neighbor, the Captain of Customs. He told us that a young flier arrived every month around the same time, stopped in Turbo overnight, and then continued on his regular route to other villages. He always bunked in with his soldiers, instead of staying at the filthy hotel in the village. He mentioned that the young man was the son of the governor of one of the Colombian states, and that he had just arrived from Cartagena, where the main office of his small airline was located.

He brought the young man out and introduced him to us. It was the young man I had seen in the village! I asked him if he had really arrived Monday morning and he later proved beyond all doubt that he had not been in Turbo Sunday afternoon, *when I saw him*. He was dressed in the same clothes on Monday as those I had seen him wearing on Sunday, in my vision.

Nostradamus, a sixteenth-century French physician, spoke of "a government of England from America" that would exist in the future, after another disastrous war. At that time the word *America* did not exist. Amerigo Vespucci had not yet made his voyage. Nostradamus also clearly described the murder of the French king Henry II. He named the man who would commit the murder, a schoolteacher, and the location of the deed. This was sixty-five years before the event —in fact, before the murderer had been born, and before the king in question had come to the throne.

Actually, this ability, found in us all, progresses from simple feelings, such as when a man senses love or warmth or danger and reacts accordingly, through intuition, in which his "inner voice" warns him of danger or somehow makes him react with caution to dangerous individuals or situations, to the higher stage, the "hunch," where actual ESP begins. A hunch is a basically *illogical* feeling about a person or situation that influences one's thinking and actions. To follow a hunch is to go against purely logical reasoning. If the hunch turns out to be correct, one has had a mild ESP experience. If the hunch turns out to be false, it may not have been a hunch at all, but fear. The two are very

much alike. Fear of failure, fear of a confrontation
that may be undesirable, frequently presents itself as a
hunch. The only way to tell the two apart is the sense
of immediacy, the sudden appearance, and the short
duration of a *true hunch*, whereas fear is a lingering
and generally somewhat extended feeling. Beyond the
simple hunch, there lies the ability to foresee or foretell
actual events or situations. Whether the foreknowledge
is of events that occur one minute later or a year later
is of no importance: the technique involved is precisely the same, since we are dealing with a dimension
in which time, as we define it, *does not exist*. The
precognitive process goes through a variety of stages or
degrees, from foretelling an encounter with either a person or a situation, without getting a specific time or
place, to actually receiving a detailed message.

A related experience is *premonition*, usually *feelings*
about events to come, rather than sharp flashes of actual
scenes. Premonitions occur more frequently than the
more complex forms of precognitive experiences. In
an article titled "Can Some People See into the Future?" published in *Family Weekly*, May 4, 1969,
Theodore Irwin reported on a London piano teacher's
strong premonition concerning the fate of Senator Robert Kennedy. Nine months before his assassination,
Mrs. Lorna Middleton felt a strong premonition that he
would be murdered. On March 15 of the year in
which Kennedy died, she actually saw the assassination
take place, and felt that it would happen while the
senator was on tour in the West. This impression was
followed by another one, on April 5, and again on
April 11, when she had a foreboding of death connected with the Kennedy family. The actual murder
took place on June 5.

As a result of people's premonitions frequently reported in the press, psychiatrist R. D. Barker set up a
Central Premonitions Registry where people could reg-
ister their feelings, toward the day when their impressions might become reality.

"Most of the premonitions come while I am working,
maybe because there is a lot of electricity at the telephone switchboard, yet they also come at night, when

the air is clear, or after a glass of wine. Usually my premonitions are accompanied by headaches, like a steel band around my forehead, but as I write them down, the headaches recede. When I feel that a premonition has been borne out, I feel utter relief. It is as if something had been bottled up in me," says Alan Henscher, British sensitive.

Mr. Henscher's most surprising premonition, made public by the British press, was related to an airplane accident. He had been awake all night due to an ominous headache, and during that period clearly foresaw an airplane crash in which there were 124 victims. The scene he saw reminded him of Greece; he sensed details of statuary around a church. The following morning he telephoned Dr. Barker with his report. Henscher instinctively felt that he was referring to Cyprus. Several weeks later there was indeed an airplane crash on Cyprus in which 124 people were killed.

Patterns of events are set in motion long before we reach their place in the time stream that some call God and others call The Law. Foreseeing events does not necessarily involve any form of spirit communication. It does not prove survival of human personality, but it does prove the existence, within man, of an extrasensory faculty that enables him, under certain conditions, to pierce the barriers of space and time, or, as it were, peek "around the edges."

Michael Bentine, a British TV star, tells of an incident he experienced. Both he and his late father, who was the Peruvian envoy to Britain, were aware of their psychic talents and inclinations. Michael was planning a trip to the northern English provinces. A few weeks before the journey, he had a vivid dream in which he saw himself driving his car at great speed; suddenly there was a sharp bend in the road, and another car's headlights appeared practically in front of him. A crash would have followed. Weeks later, when Michael had nearly forgotten this warning, he set out on his trip. It was nighttime, and he was driving on a road where he had never been before. Suddenly there was a sharp bend in the road, and Michael at once recognized the stretch of road as being identical to the one in his vision. With this realization came the memory of the rest of his dream. He slowed down immediately just in time to see the oncoming headlights of another car, which would have hit him head on, had he not been forewarned!

Not every premonition of disaster is as explicit. Sometimes it is merely an uneasy feeling of doom, but the recipient should nevertheless heed the warning. In a despatch from Miami, Florida, dated July 30, 1963, the Associated Press reported:

> Royce Atwood Wight was taking a nap in the bedroom of his small cottage but suddenly awoke and dashed out of the room.
>
> Seconds later a 36-foot, 3-ton concrete piling, which workmen had been erecting near the place, crashed through the roof.
>
> "I had a premonition of trouble," said White.

Sometimes the psychic warning is strong but not detailed enough to allow one to take steps to prevent the event. On May 28, 1963, the New York *Mirror* reported an automobile accident involving Arlene Francis, a well-known television personality:

> Arlene Francis had a premonition about her auto accident. At 12:45 P.M. Sunday she was leaving her agent, Gloria Safier's home in Quogue, Long Island. Arlene said to Gloria, "This trip is doomed. I wish I didn't have to make it." Arlene, who is one of the most sensitive and kindest people in show business, was en route to New York for her weekly *What's My Line* appearance when her car skidded out of control, hit another car, and killed a woman.

Telepathy refers to communication from mind to mind *without* the use of sensory perception. For all practical purposes, we can say that telepathy is an instant transmission of thoughts. It works best in times of stress and when the usual means of communication aren't functioning. It is particularly strong between people who have an emotional bond. The instances of mothers feeling the distress of their children, at a distance, of course, are numerous; cases where someone just has got to get through to another person, and uses his mind to send forth a message, are equally numerous and well attested to in the files of most reputable psychical research bodies, such as the American Society for Psychical Research. To a degree, telepathy can be induced experimentally. In experimental telepathy, sender and receiver should know each other in order to make the contact more possible.

Explorer Sir Hubert Wilkins and psychic Harold Sherman conducted some classic experiments in telepathy. It was agreed that Sir Hubert would mentally transmit information about himself daily from the North Pole, while Sherman was taking down whatever he received so that the material could be compared after Sir Hubert came back to New York. A team of researchers stood by Sherman in his New York hotel room, and, under test conditions, recorded the telepathic messages he received. One time, Harold Sherman insisted that he telepathically saw Sir Hubert Wilkins dancing in his evening clothes. This seemed improbable, because at the time the explorer was on an Arctic expedition. When Sir Hubert returned to New York, he was able to confirm the following: En route north, his plane had been forced to land at Calgary, Alberta, Canada, during a snowstorm. The lieutenant governor of the province happened to be in town for a ball being given in honor of a new governor general in Ottawa. He invited Sir Hubert to attend, but the explorer lacked evening clothes. Under the circumstances, the lieutenant governor loaned him a suit of tails—so what Harold Sherman had seen telepathically was indeed correct.

J.S. was born in Cleveland, graduated from college, and currently lives in California. She had an ESP incident different both from experimentally induced telepathy and from spontaneous urgency telepathy. All her life she has had ESP experiences, but this particular one was a communication between herself and a friend of hers who was asleep. "Once I was doing some research in the college library. Suddenly I heard my friend Brian call my name. I looked around but I could not find him. Then I heard him call my name again and ask if he could come in. It sounded as if he were standing right next to me. I looked at my watch for the time. When I came home I found Brian asleep on the couch. He asked me where I had been. I said, the library, then asked him where *he* had been at 2 P.M. He replied he had just gotten off work about one o'clock and had come over to see if there was anyone home at our house. He had called my name outside the house, but when no one answered, he had opened the door, called *again,* and asked if he could come in. No one was home, so he laid down on the couch."

Psychometry is the ability to touch an object and derive from it information about its owner. This is possible because emotional experiences leave an imprint upon the outer layer of the aura, or the electromagnetic field constituting the human personality. This imprint is permanent. If a "sensitive" person touches it, he will then re-create or tune in on whatever happened to the owner of the object. He will get flashes of the past, present, and even future of that person. Psychometry, or "measuring psychically," is probably the most common form of mental mediumship. However, if you try this, be sure not to try it on an object that has belonged to a number of owners, and be very careful when attempting to psychometrize antiques, such as swords or daggers—you might really be in for a shock.

Some people do not even have to touch an object to get a "reading." You can psychometrize a room. Provided you are within *reasonable* distance, you can psychometrize a particular environment. Or you can see someone, shake hands with him, and immediately get a definite impression of that person's personal "IBM card." I think we all have within us a storehouse of stimuli from birth to death, and perhaps rebirth, and a sensitive can get information from it. You probably will be able to do this with emotional images. You cannot get routine or logical things through psychometry, but very possibly you can experience flashes of emotional pictures, things that have *meaning,* whether they are happy or unhappy.

If psychometry is really at the beck and call of just about everybody, then it should also work all the time, I reasoned. I tried my hand a few times at parties, where people I had never met before made good subjects for my private "experiments." If I did not know anything about them, anything I deduced from touching an object they carried would naturally be "evidential" and not due to conscious knowledge of the person's circumstances. Although I do not claim any psychic ability beyond that which everybody has by nature, I was amazed to discover that in three out of four cases I obtained accurate details (no matter how unimportant or minor) about the person involved, thus proving to my own satisfaction that psychometry is indeed a valid form of psychic phenomena.

5
Psychic Dreams and Astral Projection

Man has always wanted to know how and why we dream, and what dreaming means in relation to the waking state. The shaman or priest of the early societies were asked these questions. However, as man became more sophisticated, he consulted his medical practitioner about his dreams, at the same time retaining the religious consultant in his life as a secondary source of information. When neither the medical nor the religious experts sufficed and his quest for a better understanding of his dreams continued, he turned to occult sources for definitions and explanations. We have long searched for the *hidden meanings* of dreams, meanings that can be explained and interpreted only by those familiar with the language of the occult.

A significant number of dreams contain material of a psychic nature, material that later becomes objective reality in the lives of those who dream it. This is common knowledge, not only among those who have studied these subjects but among laymen as well.

How do dreams come into being? According to Sandra Shulman, an English writer on the study and interpretation of dreams, dreams were originally associated with medicine and inseparably tied in with the mystic roots of civilization, magic, and religion. "Dreams might have remained in the nebulous atmosphere of poetry, superstition, and fairground quackery, but at the end of the last century a Viennese doctor,

Sigmund Freud, saw them as the keys with which to unlock the doors of man's unconscious."

I have always been fascinated by dreams, because many of my creative impulses have originated in my dreams. As I began to study dreams and their interpretations, I discovered that there are essentially two kinds of works: those by psychiatrists and psychologists, who generally deny the existence of any psychic material or explain it away on "other" (to them acceptable) grounds; and the popular "interpretations" ranging from Babylonian dreambooks to gypsy information on what to bet in the numbers game according to specific dreams the previous night.

There are four kinds of dreams: those due to physical problems, which result in nightmares or distorted imagery; dreams due to suppressed material, which are useful in psychoanalytical processes; dreams of a psychic nature; and, finally, out-of-the-body experiences, also referred to as astral projections.

Dreams due to physical discomfort or environmental pressures and those stemming from emotional difficulties are not nearly as vivid as psychic dreams or out-of-the-body experiences.

One is rarely able to "shake" psychic dreams or out-of-the-body experiences, even if one does not write them down immediately. Some psychic dreams are so strong that they awaken the dreamer. In many cases the dream remains vivid in the memory for a long time afterward. These two types of dreams occur with great frequency.

Psychic dreams contain information in the form of messages, warnings, or other communications from individual entities outside the dreamer's consciousness, or they may contain material obtained through the psychic abilities of the dreamer himself, abilities that he does not normally use when awake. A psychic dream is one in which material from an *external* source, or from an *internal* source not ordinarily active in the conscious state, is received.

Much evidence was accumulated through the mediumship of Edgar Cayce of Virginia Beach, Virginia.

Concerning dreams about the future, Dr. Harman H. Bro, in his book *Edgar Cayce on Dreams,* states that "in Cayce's view it was not only business details that would present themselves in advance to the dreamer, and that *any* condition ever becoming reality is first dreamed. He meant, of course, major developments that were the outgrowth of the directions and habits of a life or lifetimes." Cayce taught others how to dream constructively, as it were, and to recall their dreams upon awakening. Dr. Bro, in another work, *Dreams in the Life of Prayer,* says, "It was the contention of Cayce in his hypnotic state that every normal person could and should learn to recall his dreams so that he might study them for clues for better functioning in his daily life." Interestingly, Dr. Bro found that later laboratory studies of dreams uncovered a remarkable ability among some subjects to interpret their own dreams while under hypnosis. "Had Cayce done his work several decades later, he might well have been studied for his hypnotic interpretations of his own dreams, if not the dreams of others."

Ever since early man paid attention to his dreams, dreams have been considered important, but evaluations and acceptance differed from culture to culture. Rarely was there any distinction made among "true" psychic dreams, purely symbolic dreams, and experiences such as astral projection. Consequently, much significance was attached to dreams containing symbolic material that pertained solely to the individual dreamer and had no relation to the future. This went to extreme lengths: the Bible and other ancient documents are full of interpretations, in which differentiation has to be made between the dream image and its meaning in the "real" world.

The conventional scientists of today are much like the philosophers of antiquity. Aristotle could not accept the possibility that supernatural beings were in contact with men through dreams, or that the soul could detach itself from the body during sleep, as in astral projection. Conversely, almost every important ruler in ancient Greece and in the Roman Empire consulted with interpreters of dreams.

The ancients were very interested in *omens*. Omens are disguised warnings of future events, sort of a bonus for those who can read the signs and benefit from that ability. These portents are not generally clear-cut or definite, but they can be interpreted as having significance either for the one observing the omen or sometimes for entire groups of people.

Prophetic dreams are those that involve some situation or event pertaining to someone's future, and they are remembered upon awakening. Sometimes, prophetic material can also be obtained in the waking state.

In 1969, Mrs. Elaine F. of Chambersburg, Pennsylvania, had a dream in which she saw a group of people having a party. She seemed to be off "in the trees," looking on. The group was celebrating something; they seemed like Girl Scouts to her. Suddenly, some people came "out of nowhere" and began to kill the "Girl Scouts." The killers were dressed in black, and had bushy hair. In the dream, she was particularly frightened by the eyes of the leader, whom she saw clearly. When she awoke the following morning she described the scene and how she had seen blood running from the wounds of the victims. Ten days later, the Sharon Tate murders shocked the nation. As soon as Mrs. F. saw a picture of Charles Manson in the newspapers, she recognized him as the man she had seen in her dream.

On the other hand, some psychic dreams take a long time to come true. Take for instance the case of C. G. He is fifty-two, worked in New York in advertising and publishing for ten years, and currently owns his own antique-restoration business on the West Coast. Because he has had a number of paranormal dreams over the years, he began to write them down, on the chance that some of them might later become reality. In one dream, he found himself riding on a train that, as it approached a city, went underground, and finally came to a stop beside a long platform. He got off the train and walked along the platform with a large crowd of people. In the distance ahead he could see a flight of stairs; there was a light at the end, outdoors. He went upstairs and saw before him a roofed platform stretching into the distance, with railroad tracks on both sides. In his dream, he could see a large city stretching to the right horizon; but on his left he saw complete destruction—nothing but piles of rubble. He awoke, and recorded his dream. One year later, in September 1942, he went into the armed services and served in New Guinea, the Philippines, and ultimately in Japan, where he arrived in September 1945, and was stationed in a small town about thirty miles south of Tokyo. On a weekend pass he decided to take a train into Tokyo. As he approached the city, the train went underground and came to a stop beside a long platform. He joined the throng of people going to a flight of stairs ahead in the distance, and he had a strong feeling of déjà vu at the moment when he began to climb the stairs. When he arrived at the roofed platform, he recalled his dream in vivid detail. On his right stood, indeed, the intact portion of Tokyo; on his left were the results of many months of bombing by the Americans, aimed at the industrial sections of Tokyo—devastated right up to the railroad tracks.

Mrs. R. is a native of Ohio and is of Roman Catholic background. She is forty-one, the mother of three, has a happy marriage, and has received recognition for her outstanding secretarial performance from her employer, a midwestern Air Force base. Mrs. R. has had a number of ESP experiences and paranormal dreams.

In the summer of 1961 Mrs. R. had a dream two nights before a party she planned to give for her old school chums. In the dream, she saw a girlfriend whom she had not seen for three years, attending her party in a colorful dress of huge orange flower patterns on a black background. Her friend's shoulder-length hair was stringy and pushed behind her ears, and her overall appearance was quite messy. In her dream, Mrs. R. saw the group dancing on the patio when the record player changed to a twist record. When Mrs. R. started to do the twist, her girlfriend said that she knew how to do it better and proceeded to show her and the others the way her neighbor's children did the dance, and she acted like an authority on the subject.

The next morning Mrs. R. told her husband about the dream. She wondered what its significance was. When the night of the party arrived, her girlfriend came dressed *exactly* as Mrs. R. had seen her dressed in the dream. Sometime during the evening, the record player changed to a twist record, and the entire event happened exactly the way Mrs. R. had foreseen it in her dream two nights earlier.

A special category of psychic dreams are the so-called warning dreams, which allow the dreamer to take steps to avoid danger of disability.

Mrs. M. of Kentucky dreamed in July 1952 that she saw a casket in the local funeral home, and she noticed that the furniture, which had never been changed, was somewhat different from what she knew it to be. In the dream, a couch that had always faced the casket was to the right side of it. She saw her Sunday-school teacher come in, and she saw herself seated in the middle of the couch. The teacher passed to an empty spot on the left in front of her and sat down to her right. She put her arm around her and said, "I feel so sorry for you; I don't know what to do." Mrs. M. saw flowers with a large white lily cross in the middle. When she dreamed the dream a second time, she told her husband about it, remarking that she feared something might have happened to her Sunday-school-teacher's grandson, who had been seriously ill when they had left town for a short trip. She decided to write the Sunday-school teacher a letter, telling her how much she meant to her and the church and the town. When she arrived home, however, she found that her teacher's grandson was well, and so she dismissed the dream. Then, in September 1952, her dream became stark reality: she found herself at the funeral parlor in her home town, the furniture had been moved just as she had seen it in her dream, and the flowers were exactly like the large white lily cross she had seen in her dream; but her husband was in the casket, having died suddenly from a heart attack, and her old Sunday-school

teacher was comforting her, saying the same words she
had heard her speak in the dream two months prior to
the event!

Mrs. C. is a retired sales-promotion executive. In
1932 or early 1933, she is not sure which, she dreamed
that the entire department in which she worked was
being fired. She was employed as a clerk with a company associated with the New York Stock Exchange.
In the dream, all twenty people in the department were
told, one by one, that they were being fired. The
next day she told her fellow workers about it; they all
laughed. Three months later, however, the dream came
true. The entire department was eliminated and its
work absorbed by other departments. At the time of
the dream, the likelihood of this happening was extremely remote.

There is a category of psychic dreams that contain
an element of forewarning, usually of disaster or
tragedy, which *might* be avoided, if the person to whom
the warning applied could be identified, that is. In this
dream category, the identity is not given clearly, so the
connection cannot be made by the dreamer. As a result,
the dream comes true as foreseen, but leaves the
dreamer feeling helpless, and perhaps convinced that
fate has been cruel in giving him advance knowledge
of tragedy without allowing him to do something to
prevent it.

Mrs. R. of Massachusetts, fifty, is a housewife,
mother, and very shy woman. Her husband is a post-
office worker. Mrs. R. dreamed she saw a small yellow-
haired girl, about three, wearing a white dress with
small pink flowers on it. In her dream, the little girl
was standing at the curb waiting to cross the street. As
she started to cross, a black car came speeding toward
her, hitting her with such force that her body was
tossed into the air and landed many feet away. The
little girl lay there without moving and Mrs. R. knew,
in her dream, that the little girl was dead. No one
moved to touch her. After what seemed an eternity, a
shoemaker finally came out of his shop, lifted the lifeless body, and carried her to the sidewalk. The dream
ended there. However, it was so vivid that Mrs. R.

told her mother about it the next morning. All day long she thought about it at work. When she arrived home that evening, her younger brothers and sisters ran to tell her of an accident that had just happened. What they told her was exactly what she had dreamed, even to the pink and white dress, and it happened in the same spot as it had in her dream.

Telepathic, or ESP, dreams are those in which the dreamer receives information from another person, either living or dead, but pertaining to the present, even if from a distance. In telepathic dreams, the dreamer simply picks up thought energies. These transmissions need not be conscious or exact. Both actual events and contemplated events may be subjects of such dreams.

Mrs. J. W. of New Jersey had a telepathic dream. In 1941 a dear friend of hers was serving on an oil tanker based at Fort Pierce, Florida. A German submarine torpedoed this tanker at sea and all but one of the crew perished. At that time, Mrs. W. had a vivid dream in which she saw her friend trapped in his cabin; he pounded the door with his fists. She noticed the porcelain doorknob, which he kept bearing down on. Over and over, he cried out for her, calling her by his pet name for her. At this point the dream ended. Several hours later she was notified that he had died in the attack on the tanker.

Mrs. C. H. lives in Pennsylvania with her family. Her husband and three daughters are very telepathic. She has had frequent precognitive dreams for many years. "I have precognitive dreams which are sifted from the rest of my dreams by the color *green* somewhere in the dream," she explains. In February 1971 she dreamed that she saw green mountains, and several trucks sinking into the black slime that was covering the entire mountain. She saw the trucks, and suddenly found *herself* trapped deeply under the trucks and some wood. She heard herself scream until she almost lost her voice. At that moment someone called out to her, warning her that she would lose her voice. There the dream ended.

Two weeks later, the great tragedy at Aberfan, Great

Britain, shook the world: A coal slag slide had buried a schoolhouse and killed many children. The newspaper account, which reached Mrs. H. two weeks *after* her dream, stated that among other harrowing experiences, a worker had heard a child screaming, because she was trapped under the rubble. The worker called out to the child to stop screaming and asked for her name, to which she replied, Katherine. "Most experiences become a reality about two weeks after I dream them and most of them pertain to world disasters," Mrs. H. explained. "I also feel the pain of a stricken person in a tragedy." She consulted a doctor, because she did not want this talent and hoped he would rid her of it. But her psychic ability has remained with her. Mrs. H. was by no means the only one tuned in on the Aberfan disaster. A London newspaper investigated the prophetic dreams of many people who had foreseen it and described it in accurate detail.

For years I've heard mediums speak of "getting out into the astral" and flying around looking at things and people from above, and frankly, I was sure they were doing their flying in their own minds. But when Robert Monroe published his account of his amazing personal out-of-the-body experiences, I began to reconsider my position. In retrospect, I am almost sure that some of my own vivid dream experiences were in fact not dreams at all but out-of-the-body experiences, or "astral projections."

Dr. Hereward Carrington and Sylvan Muldoon's book on astral projection is the classic work dealing with this phenomenon. Experiments were set up with Dr. Carrington doing the reporting, and Muldoon, the dreaming. "Journeys Out of the Body" is an account of Robert Monroe's own experiences in this field. Mr. Monroe is a reputable scientist with a radio-engineering background.

Essentially, astral projection—also referred to as "momentary displacement"—is *inner* body (or etheric self) from the physical body, usually during sleep, but not exclusively. Astral projections have occurred in the waking condition; however, projections of any length are nearly always part of the dream experience. In this phenomenon, the sleeper travels various distances, from just to the ceiling of his room to the other side of the continent, and remains connected with his physical self by a silver cord which, however, is not always visible to him.

There are two ways to accomplish astral projection: one, willfully projecting the inner self to a predetermined location and reporting back for purposes of information or research; two, involuntary dissociation of the inner self during sleep and travel to external locations. Many or all of the events experienced in the actual state are remembered, upon awakening, with the same intensity and clarity that is typical of all truly psychic dreams.

Often, an astral projection will occur when a person has been anesthetized for surgery. These artificially induced dissociations seem to encourage astral flight, and there are many records of people describing how they watched their own operations while hovering in a corner of the ceiling above the operating table.

Mrs. P. H. of the Midwest was delivering her third baby when she began hemorrhaging and felt her inner self leave her body through her head. According to her account, she witnessed everything that happened in the delivery room, as she floated over it. Then she left the room and visited with "other souls," where she was given the choice of staying, or returning to the earth plane. She decided to return to earth, and presently awoke on the operating table, but she remembered everything she had seen when apparently "unconscious."

G. H. of North Hollywood, California, in her early forties, is the mother of two girls, ages eighteen and twenty-two, and lives with an understanding husband who is aware of her psychic experiences. On July 6, 1965, she had an extraordinary astral projection dream. At that time, her father was in the intensive care unit of the University of Minnesota Hospital. The night after her father had had a serious brain tumor removed, Mrs. H. was lying in bed at her aunt's house, where she, her mother, and other relatives were staying, in order to be closer to the hospital where her father was. Mrs. H. and her mother were talking, and they wondered what would happen if her father passed away. Suddenly, Mrs. H. began to feel completely exhausted. What happened next is a form of astral projection that differs in some aspects from the "run of the mill" astral projection experiences, and is best recorded in her own words, because her description is rather remarkable. "All of a sudden I felt a funny sensation in my toes, like a tingle, then it gradually went up to my knees and began to feel as if someone had put a plug into an electric socket and I was being electrified. The feeling went up very gradually with every part becoming electrified until it reached my head and my whole body felt like a million circuits was running through it. Then it stopped and I was looking down at myself in bed. I thought how funny I was—out, separated, and yet there was the form on the bed that was completely separated from me. I felt I was floating and thought how funny a soul could be hidden inside a body." (During this initial stage Mrs. H.'s mother kept on talking, but Mrs. H. could not hear her.)

"I started floating to my father in his hospital bed and then *went into his body*. I felt I was inside of him and could feel as he felt. I saw, through his eyes, my sister, my mother, and me beside in bed. I felt the strength of his arms squeezing to communicate. Then he spoke, using my body on the bed at my aunt's house, to say through my lips from the lifeless form on the bed that we should be strong and always stay together, the three of us, and that we needed our strength more than ever now. These words were coming from my father through my lips. Then I came out of my father's body and traveled back to my own. I entered through my head and then gradually the same process started as before, with the electricity going through the parts of my body that I was entering. I remember when I was halfway in, up to my waist, my mother was saying, What have I done to you? I tried getting back faster but I could not speak or move until I was completely inside. My body was half alive, I could not sit up. The electricity moved down to my knees and then to my toes. When I was completely in my whole body it was again as if I had a million circuits running through me. When I stopped I sat up and was able to speak. I felt as if I had slept for hours and hours, wonderfully refreshed and relaxed."

Mrs. H.'s mother confirmed that her daughter had been speaking to her, but in a voice not her own: it was as if someone else were doing the talking. At that time, Mrs. H. had not told her family about her experience.

Mrs. E. P. of San Francisco had a strange experience in 1960. One morning, just before her alarm went off, shortly before five o'clock, Mrs. P. awoke. Immediately she was aware that she was *above* her bed and looking down at her body. Then the alarm went off, and she was on her bed once more, but as she reached out to turn off the alarm, *her hand went right through the clock!* At almost the same time, she felt a jolt, and this time she could turn off the alarm.

Here are the common physical and emotional effects of astral projection:

• A feeling of extreme fatigue upon awakening, even though one may have slept for many hours, even more than usual.

• A sensation of falling down from great heights, coupled with a fear of falling, usually at the very end of each projection. This is the physical reaction as the inner self reenters the physical shell, connects with it, and assumes its lower, forward speed.

• A vivid recollection of seeing one's body below or having gone through a solid wall, usually at the beginning of a trip. Also, there are sensations of arising, drifting, gaining speed, and rapid travel to far or near destinations. A person on an astral projection is sometimes conscious of temperature changes. Some people observe a silver cord being reeled in upon their return.

• Lack of voice contact is usually experienced when the destination point is reached. Visual contact has been recorded.

• Full possession of one's reasoning faculties, i.e., the person projecting notices any changes in a scene familiar to him.

Out-of-the-body experiences occur quite frequently. All kinds of people have these experiences and find them neither dangerous nor frightening. Madame Helena Blavatsky, the late founder of the Theosophical movement, stated that astral flight was dangerous because an unwanted, potentially evil soul might enter the body of the traveler while his own soul was in flight elsewhere, but I have never heard of any such occurrence.

R. Crookall, an eminent British psychic researcher who has interpreted hundreds of cases of astral projection, says:

> In the various attempts that have been made to demonstrate the reality of out-of-the body experiences, reliance is chiefly placed on one, cases in which the claim that the person is exteriorized in a "double," or psychical body, seems to be corroborated by the fact that his apparition was seen by others, and two cases in which the experience is repeated experimentally. These evidences have not proved convincing to many.

> On the other hand, we suggest that the cumulative evidence here adduced, though necessarily of an indirect nature, serves to establish the reality of out-of-the body experiences quite as firmly as the theory of evolution is established.

Famed medium Alex Tanous recently described his experiences during astral projection:

> There were many sensations. One time I was stuck in the window, one time I was too short, one time I was way out in the oneness associated with mysticism. This oneness was like being in awe. You are not divorced from this world, don't get me wrong, it is just that suddenly the whole universe is in harmony, i.e., it is a communion with the universe. In other words, when I was out of my body the sensation was so pleasant that I didn't want to come back. Coming back takes a willful act. Somehow the mind tells me, and even before I start, I know I'm going to be coming back. My mind seems like another person. I don't

believe this is supernatural or anything else, it is merely a phenomenon of the mind that we are discovering and assuming. It is so natural to me that I never thought about it any other way.

In the Catholic religion, St. Paul refers to "in this body or out of it." Astral journeys are where many of the saints and other very highly evolved people experienced their mystical moments.

When I experience an out-of-body sensation the first thing I feel is a ball of light. This ball of light is real energy: the astral body; time and space end whenever I am doing this, past, present, or future, and I am in awe. I don't understand it. We've tested it here very scientifically.

When I am out there I feel there is no physical limitation to the distance I can travel. My other self feels so immensely free that it could do anything I wanted to do once I programmed it. It feels as though my mind is completely blank. Then the scene comes to me. For example, I was sitting here on February 11 at two-thirty in the morning. I thought of a friend of mine who is a newspaper writer in Canada, and I wanted to tell him, don't feel badly but the New Year's predictions were late and they were not printed, and that my book would be in. Two-thirty in the morning would be three-thirty in Canada. I said, all right, I knock at the door, now I'm here, the lights go on, he comes out, and we have a discussion. The dogs bark at me, everything else, and we talk and I said Ellsworth, you know, and he says, Do you want to stay overnight? What are you doing so late in the morning? You told me that anytime I was by and I'm in a hurry and I thought I'd wake you up just to say hello, all of this. I wrote this down for my good friend Dr. Osis, and went back to Maine. I get a call from this man and a letter, describing the same thing, that I was physically there and he thought I was there physically until he looked out the window and he saw no footsteps and no car. He said, I even smelled your aftershave lotion. Another member of the family also heard the knocks. He got up, and put on the light. Now there were two people recognizing the same thing. What was that other body? See, that's the astral body. Let's say that I was projected to Times Square and I would be seen there. It's certainly not a fantasy to others.

There's also some kind of telepathy between my astral body and my physical body. When I am out of my body, my physical body still speaks and relates what I am saying. Two or three groups of scientists have detected the astral body or double while I am out of the body. Since I am able to duplicate myself there's no reason that death is not actually a duplication for all or part of an everlasting life. The astral body as it leaves in death is a shapeless myth that I can only relate to energy from my outer body. Because it was visible to me at deathbeds it had to have some kind of reality. A final separation would be a big light not to this body, but one like this with mobility and everything. The out-of-the-body experience, on the other hand, combines intuition, insight, and total body experience in the act of really observing.

I have noticed, by the way, that some of my EEGs done while I am astral projecting look like a retarded child's. I am a school psychologist and have done some tests with retarded children. I found they have so much psychic ability it's unbelievable.

British parapsychologist Robert Cripall has studied thousands of cases of out-of-body experiences. He found six common denominators: First, the person feels he is leaving his body through the top of his head. I find there is no leaving through my head or eyes or anything else. I start out this way: I say, I want you to breathe, to relax and think of something extremely happy. This puts you into an alpha state for a second. Your mind is clear and blank. You think of yourself floating, like a ball of light. Then create in your third eye what you are going to send as if you were a daydreamer or an athlete about to perform. The mind knows the direction of the place where we will go.

Second, according to Cripall, at the instant of separation of the astral and physical bodies the person momentarily blacks out. For me, it is not so much a snap or break, I just feel, in the inner body, that I *was* limited, and in my outer body I am *not* limited. That's why it is an outer body. I am free to go and do anything I want. I have never seen a silver cord connecting the two. I would be afraid to be limited by it.

Three, before wandering, the astral body hovers over the physical body for a while.

Four, when the astral body returns from its travels it reenters and goes through the hovering position again.

Five, another blackout occurs at the moment of reintegration. In my case, returning to the body is the reverse of going out of the body.

Finally, Cripall says that most people experience a rapid reentry and a jolt to the physical body. Personally, I don't experience anything I would call a blackout. I do feel a timeless and spaceless sensation before I suddenly find myself back in my body.

So the next time you feel you are not quite yourself, and get that floating feeling, it may not be imaginary after all. I am assured by many in the psychic research field that projections are among the most common forms of "dissociation of personality," loosening of the bonds of consciousness, and are harmless, despite some superstitions held by certain metaphysically inclined persons. Demons do not, as a rule, wait about to enter the temporarily "empty" body of a projector, and the cases where possession by external entities occurred are extremely rare and always due to the victim's own problems or weaknesses, not to the process of astral projection itself.

6
The Case for Reincarnation

Everyday expressions such as "You only live once," "This is the only life you have—enjoy it," and "You come this way only once," are good indications that the average person considers life a unique and fleeting experience. Consequently, the fact that life is comparatively short and ends inevitably in death has given people an excuse to live lives of material enjoyment. At all times and in all civilizations, there were those who used this fundamental view of human life as an excuse to indulge in excesses of the physical pleasures of this world. To persuade them that their hedonistic approach to life was not necessarily the best one, and to consider spiritual values as well, required a powerful counterargument. This counterargument became the focal rallying point of "establishment" religion. By promising man a better life in the hereafter or resurrection at some vaguely defined future time, religion could hope to impress upon man the need for a balanced philosophy of life, in which the material and the spiritual balanced and offset each other. Only in recent years has the scientific exploration of reincarnation been pursued. Until the latter part of the nineteenth century, psychical research was in the hands of amateurs or, at times, quacks; with the emergence of an orderly scientific approach to the many phenomena of human personality now classified as ESP, the subject of reincarnation was raised. Today, after a gap of perhaps fifty years, the subject of reincarnation is again being examined, because it seems to answer so many questions left unanswered both by science and by establishment religions. Particularly among the young, the cries for information on previous and future lives are very loud, for the process of reincarnation does furnish them with an explanation for the many injustices they see all around.

Those who believe in reincarnation invoke the law of karma in order to blame even the slightest discomfort upon something they might have done in a previous existence. One has to use common sense as well as scientific appraisal to determine the validity of such theories. But it is conceivable that there exists a law, a natural law, governing all our actions, thoughts, and reactions, and that such a law might very well set up a system of retribution, of compensation, extending even to minor and seemingly unimportant details of our lives.

Reincarnation, if generally accepted as factual, would, of course, greatly influence our personal conduct. I am referring especially to conduct in times of war, under other conditions of violence, or whenever there is a possibility of taking another person's life. Whenever a man or a woman is faced with committing a crime or evil deed (I mean evil in terms of contemporary morality), there is the possibility of "accumulating karma," i.e., mortgaging one's future lifetime in a negative sense. Now, if reincarnation is subject to a universal law of retribution and justice, then an evil deed committed in one life may very well have dire consequences in the next one. The knowledge of this might influence certain people toward a better life, toward a more moral existence. It might prevent crimes of violence, perhaps even war. This may be merely wishful thinking on my part, but it stands to reason that a universally and scientifically accepted conviction that reincarnation is factual would have deep and long-lasting consequences in our way of life. The common attitude toward death, for instance, would undergo rapid and profound change, for if there is more than one life to live, surely one could not fear death as the inevitable end. Surely one might even welcome death at times, if the existence one suffers could be exchanged for a better one. The hopelessly ill particularly might well welcome a continuing life cycle.

One of the most convincing cases of reincarnation was reported by Hans Holzer in his book *Born Again,* concerning a girl who remembered life in Scotland in 1600. She had a recurrent dream:

> "The dream happened the first time about two years ago. I've had it quite a few times since then. I've seen a girl with red hair. She has a long, white gown on, and it has gold braiding on it, and she's kind of walking like she's dazed. When I have this dream I also see two towers there, and hear her say, 'Handsel to me,' and then I hear her mention 'Glamis, Angus,' and she'll say, 'Ruthven, Gowrie,' and one time she said, 'I leaped.' Sometimes she seems very peaceful and sometimes she seems very angry."

Holzer later regressed the young lady, Pamela Wollenberg, hypnotically to expand the information she remembered while fully conscious. Holzer then was able to corroborate all her statements.

> I am satisfied that Pamela Wollenberg had no access to the information she gave me when she first wrote to me. I am also satisfied that she had no ulterior motive in contacting me. No money had changed hands between us. No fame or publicity is likely to come to her. She cannot be reached, and her telephone is unlisted, so the only explanation remaining to any fair-minded individual is that Pamela Wollenberg did indeed remember a previous lifetime.

Reincarnation has always had a place in the great world religion.

The ancient Jews continually expected the reincarnation of their great prophets. To them, Moses was Abel, the descendant of Adam; and their Messiah was to be the reincarnation of Adam himself, who had already come a second time as David. It seems significant that the closing words of the Old Testament (Malachi 4:5) contain this prophecy: "Behold, I will send you Elijah the prophet before the great and terrible day of Jehovah comes."

Of course, Elijah had already lived among the Jews. But the first book of the New Testament refers to this prophecy on three occasions, thus linking the Old and New Testaments on the idea of rebirth (in the King James Version of the New Testament, the Greek form of "Elijah," namely "Elias," is used).

In the Hindu view, spirit no more depends on the body it inhabits than body depends on the clothes it wears or the house it lives in. When an outfit is too small or a house too cramped, we exchange these for roomier ones that offer our bodies freer play. Souls do the same. This process by which an individual jiva passes through a sequence of bodies is known as reincarnation or transmigration of the soul—in Sanskrit, *samsara*. On the subhuman level, the passage is through a series of increasingly complex bodies until at last a human one is attained. Up to this point the soul's growth is virtually automatic. It is as if the soul were growing steadily and normally, as a plant, and receiving at each successive stage a body that, being more complex, provides the needed room.

According to the Hindus, with the soul's graduation into a human body, this automatic ascent ends. Its assignment to this exalted habitation is evidence that the soul has reached self-consciousness, and with this estate come effort, responsibility, and freedom.

In the Koran, Islam's holy book, we read: "God generates beings, and sends them back over and over again, till they return to Him."

Granted, we proved reincarnation as factual. But what benefit is that knowledge to us? There are three tasks that lie ahead of anyone who wishes to get the full benefit of reincarnation knowledge. First, how to expand your consciousness; second, how to fulfill your life's purpose; and third, how to find out, if possible, who you were in a previous life. These three questions are basic inquiries into what you, the individual, are all about: but they are also basic questions concerning the system under which all of us operate.

Perhaps Albert Schweitzer, in expressing his belief in the "sanctity of all life," approached it more closely than any other recent contemporary. Spiritual consciousness, once accepted as a way of life, will never permit one to return to a materialistic point of view. The enlightenment stays, whether or not the individual has a successful life in the material sphere.

Reincarnation dreams are those in which the individual sees himself going through actions or in places with which he is not familiar in his conscious existence. These are psychic dreams, and all psychic dreams differ from "ordinary" dreams in precisely the same ways—by being specific and, even when fragmentary, sharp and fully remembered upon awakening. Reincarnation dreams, in particular, have a habit of coming in series, usually exact repetitions of one dream, more rarely partial repetition with follow-ups. A question often asked about this type of dream is whether it may be due to clairvoyance—a discarnate's attempt to communicate to the dreamer his or her story. This hypothesis is easily dismissed: those who experience reincarnation dreams are rarely, if ever, psychic before or after such dreams and have shown no particular talents in other areas of ESP. Also, true reincarnation dreams leave the dreamer with a feeling of restlessness, a compulsion to do something about the dream, which is not present with other types of dreams. In reincarnation dreams, the dreamer sees himself looking different from his present appearance, and yet he knows that it is himself and that it is to him that all these things are happening. With other types of psychic dreams, the dreamer himself is the observer, not the participant, except of course with precognitive dreams, in which he may appear in the dream as his present self, looking exactly as he does when he goes to bed. But reincarnation dreams always deal with the past, therefore the dreamer never looks the way he does in his present life.

Conventional psychiatrists may dismiss such dreams as fantasies, wish-fulfillment dreams, meaningless romanticizing of present-day events, and altogether connected with the personality of the dreamer without containing so much as an ounce of information from the dreamer's earlier lives. They do not accept reincarnation as a valid theory, despite the number of verified reincarnation dreams on record. When the dreamer awakens and remembers a dream in which he saw himself as a different person in a different age, when he remembers names and circumstances from a past with which he is not familiar in his present life and to which he has no access, if he wanted to research it, and when such material is subsequently proven to be authentic, and the personality referred to by the dreamer actually existed, then it is very difficult indeed to blame it all on the personality quirks of the *present* person.

Reincarnation memories come to some people at various times in their lives, but most of us have never had them. It is my conviction, from the studies I have undertaken, that only where a previous life has been in some way cut short, has been tragic, is the individual given part of the memory, as a sort of bonus to influence him in his present conduct. People who had full lives prior to their present one never remember those prior lives, neither in dreams nor in so-called waking flashes, nor in a déjà vu, which is a phenomenon sometimes related to reincarnation memories. Most of the déjà vu phenomena are simply precognitive experiences that are not realized at the time they occur but are remembered when the knowledge gained through precognition becomes objective reality. Some déjà vus, especially those that are complex and contain precise and detailed information about places and situations the perceiver is not familiar with, are due to reincarnation memories. All déjà vu experiences occur in the waking state, but they are related to reincarnation dreams in that they also disclose to the individual some hidden material from his own past.

Where, then, does one draw the line between fantasy dreams and material capable of verification? As with all dreams, we must take into account the individual's background, education, ability to involve himself in the subject of his dreams, and other personal factors that differ from individual to individual. Let us assume that someone dreams of a life in ancient Egypt, but has a working knowledge of Egyptology, or perhaps a personal interest in it. In this case, was the dream material suggested by the dreamer's conscious knowledge, flushed out as cleverly as the unconscious is able to, or are we dealing here with reincarnation? Are memories of a previous life in ancient Egypt *causing* the dreamer in his current life to pursue a study of that period?

Professor Holzer reported the amazing case of June Weidermann, a professional nurse who has long had an active interest in parapsychology. In his book *The Psychic Side of Dreams,* she is shown to be one of the few people who combine ESP ability with some reincarnation dreams.

When June was seven years old she suddenly seemed to "wake up" and had a distinct feeling of being in a strange place with strange people. For about six months she was convinced that her parents were not her parents at all, because of their peculiar *round* eyes—which seemed strange to her. Finally, her mother had had enough, and showed her newspaper clippings announcing her birth, and her birth certificate, to convince her that she was really their daughter!

This indeed convinced June, but about that time she had a recurrent dream concerning a household compound in a house in China. All she could ever see was the bare compound laid with large, flat stones and a wall of the same material. In the center was a tree that sometimes had beautiful blossoms and sometimes was bare and covered lightly with a layer of snow. There was no one else there but herself. At the same time, she became aware of a certain perfume that surrounded her. This particular odor would always bring to mind the words "ming tree," although she did not at the time know what ming trees were. The Oriental dream was rather comforting to Mrs. Weidermann, and in this life she has grown more and more fond of Oriental things.

However, she has had two other recurrent dreams, which are more disturbing. In one of them she is a young man wearing rubber britches, standing on top of a crude ladder that is leaning against a high wall. It is night; the ground below her falls away from the ladder, and she finds herself slowly falling backward, still holding tightly to the top rung of the ladder. She usually jerks herself awake from this dream, but sometimes, just before she hits the ground, she thinks to herself, still in the dream, "Oh, no, not again!" The night is always dark, but there is moonlight or some other source of light, for she can see herself falling away from the wall and finds herself trapped under the ladder on the ground.

In still another dream, she sees a house in the distance, and runs toward it, happy that she is home at last. She sees herself going up to a porch and notices long glass windows on each side of the door. She enters, but the house is bare. She steps down two stairs into a room off the foyer. There she sees a rather dilapidated staircase, and a long room with a bay window to the right. When she has this dream, she has also occasionally seen antique furniture in the room, but usually she sees a threadbare rug on the floor and an empty room. The dream ends there. She has never been in such a house in this life. The dream does not unduly upset her, as does the one in which she falls off the ladder. Being a trained nurse and a well-read psychical researcher, Mrs. Weidermann has long since learned to cope with her reincarnation dreams.

It is rare, however, that a person can recollect large segments of an earlier existence in the physical world, and it is even rarer that they recollect their earlier lives from the beginning—that is to say, from birth onward. Occasionally there are cases of recollections in which the person does actually recall his or her own birth. In general, average people may remember as far back as their early school years.

Typical is the case of Mrs. N. A. She is twenty-six-years old, a licensed practical nurse, and she is married to a professional musician. They have one son and live in a city in Alabama. Her interests are music and the arts. She and her husband enjoy reading books, but they have never had any particularly strong interest in the occult or in psychic research. Ever since she was a

small child and able to speak, Mrs. A. had insisted to
her mother that she did recall the moment of her birth
into this world. She vividly described the day she was
brought home from the hospital—a sixteen-day-old
baby.

> My birth memories consist of an awareness of being
> blasted into a place where extremely bright lights and
> what seemed like the resounding echoes of human
> voices were imposed on my small person. I vaguely
> seemed to remember a detached observance of this
> affair, including blurred visions of figures clothed with
> masks and caps. The day I was brought home I re-
> member riding snuggled in the arms of a woman with
> light brown hair and a prominent nose, arriving at a
> house where my aunt Jeff and sixteen-month-old
> brother were coming out the front door, onto the
> front porch, I suppose to greet my mother and me. I
> do remember it was the first time I had seen trees, and
> I was impressed by them. More clearly than anything
> is my memory of observing my mother, and in the
> thought language of the newborn, wondering, Who
> is she? What am I, and who are those people standing
> on the porch? Since I was a young child I have al-
> ways had the feeling of total detachment from myself
> and others, as if I were on the outside looking in.

Ordinary memories fade in time, and so it is not surprising that reincarnation memories might also fade as
time goes on. It is therefore rather interesting to study
the cases of young children having such memories,
which in later life usually disappear from their conscious minds. A good case in point is that of Mrs.
Carole Hardin of Montana. Mrs. Hardin lives with her
husband, who works in one of the local mines.

Nothing very special happened with little Brenda,
one of their children, until Good Friday of 1969. On
that day, Brenda sat up, awakening from a sound
sleep, and started to talk about a previous life. According to Hans Holzer, the little girl said, "I have lived
in the country once, in the South, in a big, white house."
She then went on to describe it as having had a big

porch with white pillars and a big, green lawn. She referred to a pet horse named Hooper John, which she seemed rather fond of. She was asked if there were any other children. "Yes," the girl said, "a lot of little darkies." She spoke with a strong accent, apparently French, and gave her name, which was a French name. Finally, the little girl added, "But I died." Her family thought that they had misunderstood her and asked what she had said. "I died," the little girl repeated somewhat impatiently. "I fell off my horse, Hooper John, when I was sixteen, and I died." She then lay back down and went back to sleep.

In researching the field of reincarnation, I discovered that authoress Joan Grant, married to Dr. Denys Kelsey, a psychiatrist, was able to trace her own earlier lives:

I was twenty-nine before I managed to recover the technique of being able to relive an earlier incarnation in detail and as a deliberate exercise. Until then, my conviction that I had had many lifetimes before I was born of English parents, in London, on the twelfth of April 1907, was based on disjointed episodes from seven previous lives, four male and three female. These episodes, although as natural as memories from more immediate yesterdays, were frustrating, because I could not fill in the gaps in continuity which would have linked them into coherent sequences.

As far as I have been able to discover, it is no more difficult to recall an episode that took place several millennia ago than to recall one from the current or the preceding century. Ms. Grant speaks of her "return" to Egypt in 1935, annoyed "that certain avenues of trees no longer led from Hat-shepsut's temple to Karnak, and feeling depressed that there were so many ruins instead of being pleased that there was so much left to see. I had no intimations that I had spent the best part of two thousand years in the Nile Valley. Eighteen months later, through the trivial catalyst of psychometrizing a scarab, I did the first of the 115 total recalls which became a posthumous autobiography of over 120,000 words."

All great philosophers accepted reincarnation as natural. Victor Hugo said, "The tomb is not a blind alley; it is a thoroughfare. It closes on the twilight, it opens on the dawn."

7
Ghosts and How to Deal With Them

A ghost, according to famed "ghosthunter" Professor Hans Holzer, is a surviving emotional memory of people who have died tragically and are unaware of their own passing. A ghost is a split-off personality that remains behind in the environment of the person's previous existence, whether a home or place of work, but closely tied to the spot where the person actually died. Ghosts do not travel, do not follow people around, and they rarely leave the immediate vicinity of their tragedy. Once in a while, a ghost will roam a house from top to bottom, or may be observed in a garden or adjacent field. But they do not ride in cars or get on buses, they do not appear at the other end of town: those are *free* spirits, who are able to reason for themselves and to attempt communication with the living.

In the mind of the casual observer, of course, ghosts and spirits are the same thing. Not so to the trained parapsychologist, I discovered. Ghosts are similar to psychotic human beings: incapable of reasoning for themselves or taking much action. Spirits, on the other hand, are the surviving personalities of all of us who die in a reasonably normal fashion. A spirit is capable of continuing a full existence in the next dimension, to think, reason, and feel and act, while his unfortunate colleague, the ghost, can do none of those things. All a ghost can do is repeat the final moments of his passing, the unfinished business, as it were, over and over until it becomes an obsession. In this benighted state

he is incapable of much action, and ghosts are therefore nearly always harmless. In the handful of cases in
which ghosts seem to have caused people to suffer, there
was a previous relationship between the person and the
ghost. In one case, someone slept in a bed in which
someone else had been murdered, and was mistaken by
the murderer for the same individual. In another case,
the murderer returned to the scene of his crime and
was attacked by the person he had killed. But by and
large, ghosts do not attack people, and there is no danger in observing them or having contact with them, *if*
one is able to.

The majority of ghostly manifestations draw upon
energy from the living in order to penetrate our three-
dimensional world. Other manifestations are subjective,
especially when the receiver is psychic. In that case,
the psychic person hears or sees the departed individual in his mind's eye only, while others cannot observe it.

Ghosts—that is, individuals unaware of their own
passing or incapable of accepting the transition because of unfinished business—make themselves known
to living people at frequent, usually unpredictable intervals. There is no sure way of knowing why some
individuals make postmortem appearances and others
do not. It seems to depend upon the intensity of feeling, the residue of unresolved problems, which they
have within their system at the time of death. Consequently, not everyone who dies a violent death becomes
a ghost; far from it. If it were otherwise, our battle-
fields and other horror-laden places, such as concentration camps and prisons, would indeed be swarming
with ghosts, but they are not. It depends on the attitude
of the individual at the time of death, whether the passing is accepted and the person proceeds to the next
stage of existence, or whether he is incapable of realizing that a change is taking place and consequently
clings to the physical environment with which he is
familiar, the earth sphere.

In researching many books on ghosts, such as Suzy
Smith, James Reynolds, and Desmond Leslie, I realized
two of the most common misconceptions about

ghosts: they appear only at night, and that they eventually fade away as time goes on. To begin with, ghosts are split-off personalities incapable of realizing the difference between day and night. They are always in residence, so to speak, and can be contacted by properly equipped mediums at all times. They may put in appearances only at certain hours of the day or night, depending upon the environment; for the fewer physical disturbances there are, the easier it is for them to make themselves known to the outer world. They are dimly aware that there is something out there that is different from themselves, but their diminished reality does not permit them to fully grasp the situation. Consequently, since quiet moments are more likely to occur at night than in the daytime, the majority of reported sightings occur at night.

Some manifestations occur at the exact moment of the death anniversary, because at that time the memory of the unhappy event is strongest. But this does not mean that the presence is absent at other times—it is merely less capable of manifestation. Because a ghost is not only an expression of human personality left behind in the physical environment but no longer part of it, but is in terms of physical science an electromagnetic field uniquely impressed by the personality and memories of the departed one, it represents a certain energy imprint in the atmosphere and, as such, it cannot simply fade into nothingness. Professor Albert Einstein has demonstrated that energy can never dissipate, only transmute into other forms. Ghosts do not fade away over the centuries; they are present for all eternity, unless someone makes contact with them through a trance medium and brings reality to them, allowing them to understand their predicament and thus free themselves from their self-imposed prison.

According to Peter Underwood, renowned head of the London Ghost Club:

There are more ghosts seen, reported, and accepted in the British Isles than anywhere else on Earth. I am often asked why this is so and can only suggest that a unique ancestry with Mediterranean, Scandinavian,

Celtic and other strains and intrinsic island detach-
ment, and enquiring nature, and perhaps our readiness
to accept a supernormal explanation for curious happenings may all have played their part in bringing
about this state of affairs.

Of course, there are such famous places as Hampton
Court, which is just filled with specters. The spirit of
King Henry VIII seems to brood heavily over the mel-
low Tudor palace itself. He was at Hampton with five
of his six wives, and it was there, on October 12, 1537,
that his third queen, Jane Seymour, bore him a son and
died a week later. Her ghost walks here, or rather
glides, clad in white, perambulating the Clock Court.
Carrying a lighted taper, she has been seen emerging
from a doorway in the Queen's Old Apartments, wandering noiselessly about the stairway and through the
Silver Stick Gallery. Quite recently some servants
handed in their notice because they had seen "a tall
lady, with a long train and a shining face" walk through
closed doors, holding a taper, and glide down the stairs.

The famous White Lady of Hampton Court is reputed to haunt the area of the landing stage, and a number of anglers reported seeing her one midsummer night
a few years ago. There is also the ghost of Archbishop
Laud (whose spirit is also said to appear in the library
of St. John's College, Oxford, rolling his head across the
floor!), which allegedly has been seen by residents at
the palace, strolling slowly without a sound (but complete with head!) in the vicinity of the rooms he once
knew so well.

Lady Catherine Howard is perhaps the most famous
ghost of Hampton Court. In 1514 she came here, a
lovely girl of eighteen, as the bride of the fat, lame,
aging monarch. A year after her arrival, ugly rumors
began to circulate that described her behavior before
and after her marriage as a little better than a common
harlot's. The night before she was arrested, her first
step to the block, she broke free from her captors and
ran along the gallery in a vain effort to plead for her
life with her husband. But Henry was piously hearing
vespers in the chapel and ignored her entreaties, and

she was dragged away, still shrieking and sobbing for mercy. As you go down the Queen's Great Staircase you can see on the right-hand side the low-roofed corridor containing the room from which Queen Catherine escaped and to which she was dragged back, her screams mingling weirdly with the singing in the chapel. Her ghost reenacts this event on the night of the anniversary, running shrieking through what has become to be known as "haunted gallery." Those who have heard and seen her ghost include Mrs. Cavendish Doyle and Lady Eastlake, together with many servants at the palace. All the witnesses say that the figure has long, flowing hair, but usually the apparition disappears so quickly that no one has time to observe it closely.

The common term *poltergeist,* which is German for "noisy ghost," used to be applied mainly to physical phenomena occurring in haunted houses. These phenomena—such as objects moving mysteriously by themselves, flying through the air without apparent natural cause, and clearly defined noises such as heavy thumpings—are noticeable to all, not just to the psychic person.

It was believed that the presence of a child below the age of puberty was necessary to cause these phenomena, and that, indeed, the youngster unconsciously created them by the force of his untapped libido. It was felt that it was a young person's way of expressing himself and of getting attention from the family that might have been lacking. This old view of poltergeist phenomena still prevails in German parapsychological circles, since it obviates the need for the researcher to admit evidence of extrahuman interference, and thus makes him breathe easier when he faces his board of directors or other skeptics.

But it does not correspond to the facts, at least not to all the facts. In some cases, the actions of a retarded person may cause objects to fly. I am convinced that the presence of a child or of a retarded adult can indeed furnish the force necessary to accomplish these seeming contradictions of natural law. But in the majority of cases I have researched, I have found indications that this force is used by an intelligent, if warped, nonphysical entity *outside* the child's mind. The youngster is the tool, not the creator of the disturbances.

M.D., a medical journal, had this to say about poltergeists, in an article published in February 1964:

> The strangest aspect of poltergeist manifestation is the violation of ballistic principles: dozens of bemused observers have noted thrown objects traveling at unnaturally slow speeds and along impossibly curved paths, even circles; objects also hover motionless and make such soft landings that not even fragile china is broken. In a celebrated case in England in 1849, witnesses swore they saw salt and pepper emerge from their respective shakers, whirl and mix in the air like a swarm of bees and return, unmixed, to their proper receptacles.

Poltergeist-propelled objects are frequently found to be warm or hot on landing, even in Iceland and Siberia.

Psychical researchers use the term recurrent spontaneous psychokinesis (RSPK), and believe that the phenomena are usually associated with a child or young adult. In one study of poltergeist cases, more than three fifths of the manifestations were associated with a "central body," most of whom were females; in all but five instances the central party was under twenty; the average age was thirteen years for boys, fourteen for girls.

Not all investigators agree that some naughty boy or girl is consciously responsible; some feel that the children are actually possessed by the spirit and carry out its pranks unconsciously, being gifted for the time being with something approaching criminal cunning.

In the famous case at Stratford, Connecticut, in 1850, a poltergeist plagued Presbyterian clergyman Dr. E. Phelps and his progeny for eighteen months, smashing chairs and breaking candlesticks. The son (twelve) and daughter (sixteen) were pelted with stones and clods of earth, tossed in the air, and the boy's pants were pulled off.

Although poltergeist phenomena occur quite frequently, today's ordinary observer is just as baffled by them as were his ancestors. A typical case was reported in the *Los Angeles Times* of November 11, 1962, by reporter Charles Davis, who witnessed the incident at Big Bear City, California:

Don Beasley, 20-year-old student, described Saturday how he watched in amazement as stones floated down out of the sky and landed on a cabin and the ground around it.

First public disclosure of the phenomenon was made Friday.

Beasley and John Holdorf, former Redlands student, moved into the cabin after it was vacated by Mr. and Mrs. W. M. Lowe and their five children. The cabin is at 301 Division Rd.

Beasley, who is employed with Holdorf at the nearby Rebel Ridge Ski area, said they had dinner with the Lowes in the cabin before they moved and were told jokingly that the house was haunted.

"Then the stones started falling," said Beasley, "and I couldn't believe it.

"I thought at first maybe kids were throwing these stones, but then I saw that wasn't possible. The stones were coming straight down from the sky. The stones actually seemed to float down. One guy was standing outside and one of the stones hit him on the arm but it didn't hurt him. They didn't hit hard.

"One time my car was hit while I was standing right beside it. I had the sunroof open and I heard a plunk. I found the rock on the seat."

Not all ghostly manifestations have physical aspects. In fact, most ghosts restrict themselves to visual phenomena such as apparitions, or to auditory experiences such as footfalls, voices, and miscellaneous noises of human presence, which may be re-creations of noises heard when the ghost was actually in his physical body or at the time of his death. Chills, unexplained cold spots, and drafts are also part of the sensory experiences connected with hauntings. These are by no means created by Dracula-like ghosts to frighten people, but are natural phenomena due to the presence of psychic energy or electromagnetic fields. Whenever a ghost is present in a house, the area of main activity may feel clammy, and even people who have no psychic talents whatever will feel this.

Others complain of shivers and a sense of bodily chill. These experiences are not due to fear or imagination, as one might quickly assume; they are uncontrolled natural reactions to a change in the atmosphere of a room or an entire house. Most important, these changes can be measured by sensitive instruments designed to record temperature fluctuations and electromagnetic disturbances.

I discovered that in at least one case, a ghostly presence was proved by a Geiger counter in the hands of a totally skeptical engineer. When he approached the area of the room in which the alleged ghost was standing, his instrument indicated radiation in the area. There was no other explanation for this result, and the engineer is a little less sure of his prejudices now.

Hans Holzer reported one of the most evidential cases of a ghost hunt in his 1963 book, *Ghost Hunter*. A gentleman who eventually identified himself as General Samuel Edward McGowan of the Confederate Army claimed to have been murdered, or at least attacked, in a certain house on New York's lower Fifth Avenue, where his ghost had been observed by some tenants. Through the mediumship of Ethel Meyers, he divulged so many intricate details of the Civil War that only an expert on the subject could have known them.

Mrs. Meyers, a vocal coach, was not qualified to undertake such research, even if she had wanted to do so in order to defraud the researchers. None of them had any knowledge of the subject beyond rudimentary outlines of the period. Yet, names of company commanders, skirmishes, a duel and how it ended, and many other personal details of the life of the general were brought out in the trance and later verified.

During one of the seances, the communicator, now no longer a ghost, but freed from his original abode and obsessions and free to talk, stated that he had paid his rent not to his landlady, whom he identified as

Ghosts

In Search of
Strange
Phenomena

the main floor above his head. He allegedly became so upset that he almost electrocuted himself at the switches!

Ghosts and hauntings occur to people in all walks of life. Mrs. S. F. of central Pennsylvania is a middle-aged divorcée. She works in an assembly plant, assembling electronic parts, had an average education, and is a native of Pittsburgh, where her father worked for a steel company. She has several brothers and sisters.

She knew she was psychic, but paid little attention to her "special" gift. It was only when she moved into a certain house that the matter took on new aspects.

Mrs. F., who lived alone, moved into a compact two-story house connected to four similar houses by what is locally called a party wall: two houses sharing the same wall. The front door opens into the living room, beyond which is the kitchen. There are two rooms downstairs, two bedrooms upstairs, and the bathroom is in the cellar. The house next door is similar and belonged to a widow. Next to that is another, similar house, in which some of this widow's family lived at the time Mrs. F. moved into her house. There were four houses in all, and when she saw them, the four houses seemed to share a common ground.

She discovered that the back bedroom was too cold in the winter and too hot in the summer, so she decided to switch from one bedroom to the other depending on the temperature. One spring night while sleeping in the back bedroom, she awoke from a sound sleep to see a man bending over her, close to her face. He had a ruddy complexion, a high forehead, and was partly bald with white hair around his ears. He gave her a cold stare and then faded away. Mrs. F. thought she had had a hallucination or had dreamed the whole thing, so she went back to sleep. Another night Mrs F. was in bed reading, when she suddenly heard a swish-like sound, and a thump. At the same time, something punched her bed and hit her in the head. She clearly felt a human hand near her eye, but could not see anything. A few days later, when she was reading again in the late hours of the night, she noticed the bed go down as

"Elsie," but to her handyman, Pat Duffy. The year, he claimed, was 1873.

Several days *after* this disclosure, Holzer was able to establish that the house in question had belonged to a woman only once, in 1873, and that her name had been Isabella Clark (Isabella is a variation of Elizabeth, as is Elsie). Searching further, he found in contemporary city records that both Isabella Clark and Patrick Duffy, laborer, were registered at the same address, 45 Cherry Street, New York!

The Octagon, now the American Institute of Architects, in Washington, D.C., served as temporary White House after the British had burned down Washington in the early nineteenth century.

A Colonel Tayloe had built the mansion primarily for his daughter, but she disgraced him by bringing home the "wrong" kind of husband. Father said "no" and daughter committed suicide by jumping from the third floor and landing smack in front of the staircase. For years people have observed ghostly happenings in the building. The one-time curator, Mrs. May, has seen the big chandelier swing of its own volition and has heard all sorts of noises when she knew positively that there was no one but herself in the building. Once she accompanied porters Allen and Bradley to the top floor, long closed to the public and deeply covered with dust. Nevertheless, they plainly saw the impressions of human feet leading to the spot from which the girl had jumped to her death.

The skeptical superintendent of the institute, Alric H. Clay, was driving by the building with his family one night, when he noticed the lights inside ablaze. Having locked up just a few hours before, he was concerned. He entered the building and found all the locks undisturbed. But the carpet edge was flipped back on the very spot where the girl had landed in death. Clay did not believe in ghosts. He went upstairs, inspected all the floors, turned the carpet back, and then proceeded to the basement, where the light switches are. At that moment he clearly heard someone walk on

Hans Holzer, a ghost hunter,
explores this strange phenomenon scientifically.
He says a ghost is a surviving emotional
memory of one who has died tragically and is
unaware of his own passing.

This house in Port Clyde, Maine, was investigated by Hans Holzer in 1976. Once he had established that the house was haunted, his job was to find out who the ghost was and put it to rest.

The Washington Irving house, "Sunnyside," located in Tarrytown, New York, is reputed to be haunted.

Psychic
Photography

Dr. Thelma Moss, Department of Clinical Medicine, UCLA, does research with a Kirlian camera.

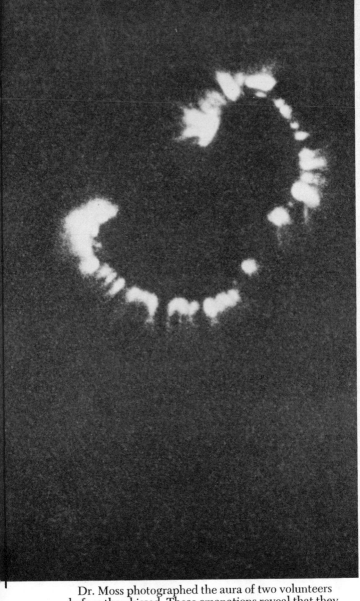

Dr. Moss photographed the aura of two volunteers before they kissed. These emanations reveal that they are certainly communicating on a nonverbal level.

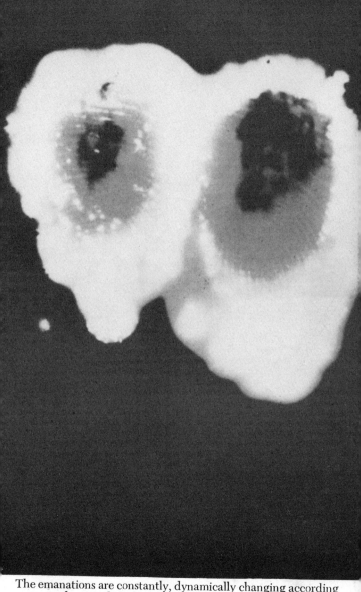

The emanations are constantly, dynamically changing according
to the way the subject responds to his environment.
This is the aura of a man under the influence of marijuana.

Plant
Sentience

Lie-detector expert Cleve Backster started the current trend of scientific investigation into plant communication.

Backster attached the electrodes of one of his machines to a plant. He then asked a woman seated nearby, her age and she lied.
The polygraph registered a lie.

Dorothy Retallack, under controlled conditions, played acid rock music to one group of plants and semi-classical music to another. The plants visibly leaned away from the

rock music and toward the classical as if to draw strength. Plants do respond dramatically to certain sounds.

Pyramid Energy

The Giza complex.
The pyramid shape produces an energy field that is
beneficial to the human body. It is
claimed that it can heal sore areas as well as increase
vitality and productivity.

Inside the King's chamber
bodies become naturally mummified.
The pyramid form
can alter and change energy.

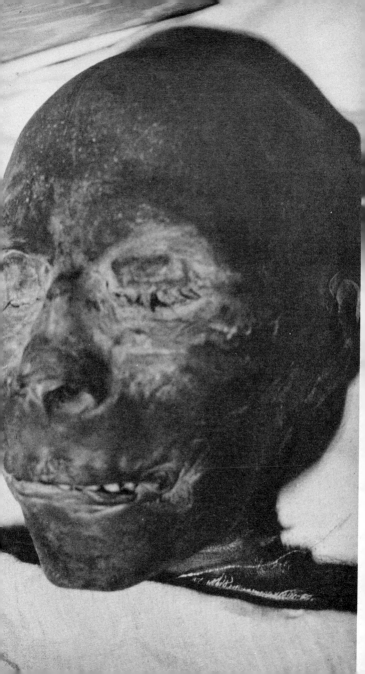

Archaeological
Puzzles

The Colossus of Memnon, the vocal statue,
emitted sounds at rare intervals from 20 B.C. to 196 A.D.—
always at sunrise. It appeared to exercise
some strange inherent power of saluting the sun.

The mysterious race that preceded the Incas were not only
able to cut and fit enormous monoliths, but they

somehow carried the blocks incredible distances depositing
them on mountaintops such as Ollantayparubo, Peru.

When the Spaniards arrived at Tiahuanaco,
the Aymara Indians they found were unable to tell them
much about the vast deserted
city except that it had been built by the gods.

Karen Getsla,
a psychic, read the past of
Tiahuanaco and described
how the massive
boulders were cut and fit.
A secret ingredient,
a radioactive plant extract,
dissolved stone
so that it made the edges
malleable and fuse together.

Ruins found in the Pacific have given rise to
popular speculation that such islands must be the remains
of another lost continent. Such a continental

land mass must have existed to explain the hundreds of
cyclopean statues on Easter Island.

The
Mysterious
Bermuda
Triangle

Frank Flynn survived an unexplainable incident
in the Triangle in 1956 while on duty aboard the *Yamacroft*.
The ship encountered a
thick, gray mass on a clear calm night.

Bob Spielman loaned his Beachcraft Bonanza to some friends
who flew out into the direction of the
Grand Bahama Island. They suddenly lost radio contact
with Miami and never arrived at their
destination. Investigations revealed that the wing had
been completely wrenched off the plane
by an unexplainable force.

Carlton Hamilton, an airport traffic controller
in Florida, believes that there is some strange phenomenon

that happens up to 150 miles off the Florida
coast and between the altitude of 10,000 feet to sea level.

Life
After
Death

Sheldon Ruderman has had two near-death
experiences accompanied by out-of-body experiences (OBE).
His first OBE occurred after an 8-hour operation
to remove a cancerous right lung. His desire to see his
second operation was realized by an OBE.

Dr. Charles Garfield of the Cancer Research Institute
of the University of California believes
out-of-body experiences warrant serious study.

if someone were sitting on it. It clearly showed the indentation of a human body, yet she could not see anything. She also heard a man's voice, coming to her as if from an echo chamber. It sounded like a muffled "hello."

Mrs. F. never felt comfortable in the back bedroom, so she decided to move permanently into the front room. One night when she was in bed in that room, her eyes opened and rested on a cupboard door across from the bed. This time she clearly saw the dark silhouette of a man. His most outstanding features were his burning eyes and strange, pointed ears. When he saw her looking at him, he moved back into the door and disappeared.

Again, Mrs. F. refused to acknowledge that she had seen a ghost, and thought it was all a hallucination, as she had been awakened from a deep sleep. A few minutes later, she decided she wanted a snack. She got up to get some potato chips, and as she rounded the bend of the hall she happened to glance at the wall—and there was that same man again. She could clearly make out his face and pointed ears. As soon as the ghost realized that she had discovered him, he quickly moved back into the wall and disappeared. Clearly, the apparition was *not* a hallucination, since she was fully awake and therefore could not blame her dreams for it.

While she was still wondering what this all meant, she had another, similar experience. She was back in bed, reading, when she thought she heard something move in the kitchen. A little later she decided to go down to get a fruit drink. The hall lights were on, so the kitchen wasn't completely dark. Just the same, when she reached the kitchen she turned on the light. As soon as she did so, she saw the same ghostly apparition, standing there in the kitchen, only this time she could see his entire body. He wore pants, a shirt with a collar, and rounded-toe shoes. He had curly hair, a straight nose, and full lips. She noted particularly the full lips and, of course, the pointed ears. As soon as he noticed her, he ran into the wall and disappeared. But she noticed that his legs started to shake when the light went on, as if he was trying to get going and didn't quite know how. Then he hunched over a little, and shot into the wall.

Mrs. F. was shocked. She shut off the light and went back to bed. Eventually she drifted off to sleep again. The entire incident puzzled her, for she had no idea who the ghost might be.

One day soon after this experience, she was leaving her house, and as she passed her neighbor's house, she noticed a young man sitting on the steps, looking out into the street. She saw his profile, and like a flash it went through her mind that it was the same profile as that of the ghost she had seen in her kitchen! She looked again, and sure enough, there were the same full lips and the same pointed ears.

Immediately, she decided to discuss the matter with a neighbor who lived at the end of the street. She was a good person to talk to, because she understood about such matters. In fact, Mrs. F. had spent a night at this neighbor's house once when she was particularly upset by the goings-on in her own house. The neighbor assured her that the widow's son—the young man she had seen sitting on the steps—was the "spitting image" of his father. Mrs. F. had not seen him before because he was married and lived elsewhere, and had just been visiting his mother that day.

Well, Mrs. F. put two and two together, and realized that the ghost she had seen was her late neighbor. On making further inquiries, she discovered that the man had suffered from rheumatic fever, and had been in the habit of lying on a couch to watch television. One day his family had awakened him so that he wouldn't miss his favorite program. At that moment he had a heart attack, and died, right there on the couch.

Not all ghostly visitors are frightening or represent negative influences. Take the case of Mrs. M. N. In 1939 she leased a lovely, old three-story house on Commerce Street in New York's Greenwich Village.

Mrs. N. loved the house like a friend; as she was at that time going through a personal crisis in her life, a group of friends, who were many years younger than she, moved into the house with her. Before actually moving into the house, Mrs. N. had met one of her neighbors, who was astonished that she had taken this particular house.

"For goodness' sake," the neighbor said, "why are you moving in *there?* Don't you know that place is haunted?"

Mrs. N. and her friends laughed at the thought, having not the slightest belief in the supernatural. Several days before the furniture was to be moved into the house, the little group gathered in the bare living room, lit their first fire in the fireplace, and dedicated the house with prayers. It so happened that they all were followers of the Bahai faith, and they felt that prayer was the best way to create a harmonious atmosphere in what was to be their new home.

They had been in the empty living room for perhaps an hour, praying and discussing the future, when suddenly there was a knock on the door. Dick, one of the young people who was nearest the door, went to answer the knock. There was no one there. Fifteen minutes later they heard another knock. Again, there was no one outside. The knocking sounded once more that night. Just the same, they moved in, and almost immediately heard the footsteps of an unseen person. There were six living in the house at the time. The first time they heard the steps, they were all at dinner in the basement dining room. The front door, which was locked, opened and closed, and footsteps were heard going into the living room, where they seemed to circle the room, pausing now and then.

Immediately Dick went upstairs to investigate, and found no one about. Despite this, they felt no sense of alarm. Somehow they knew that their ghost was benign. From that moment on, the footsteps of an unseen person became part of their lives. They checked every strange occurrence, but there was nobody to be seen, and eventually they realized that whoever it was that was sharing the house with them preferred to *remain* unseen.

Since there were no other uncanny phenomena, the group accepted the presence of the ghost without undue alarm. One night, however, a group of Bahai

Youth were invited to stay with them, and as a result Mrs. N. had to sleep on the couch in the basement dining room. It turned into a night of sheer terror for her; she didn't see anything, but somehow the terror was all around her like thick fog. She didn't sleep a moment that night. The following morning, Mrs. N. queried a girl named Kay, who ordinarily slept on the basement couch, as to whether she had ever had a similar experience. She had not. However, a few days later, Kay reported a strange dream she had had while occupying the basement couch.

She had been awakened by the sound of the door opening. Startled, she had sat up in bed, and watched, fascinated, as a group of Indians filed through the door, walked along the end of the dining room, and went through the kitchen and out the back door, where she could hear their feet softly scuffing the dead leaves! They paid no attention to her at all, but she was able to observe that they were in full war paint.

Since Kay had a lively imagination, Mrs. N. dismissed the story. As there were no further disturbances, the matter of the ghost receded to the backs of their minds. One morning about a year after they had moved into the house, Mrs. N. had to catch an early train, and not having an alarm clock herself, asked Dick to set his alarm clock and wake her.

Promptly at six A.M. there was a knock at her door, to which Mrs. N. responded, "Thanks," and just as promptly went back to sleep. A few minutes later there was a second knock on the door, to which she replied that she was getting up. Later, she thanked her friend for waking her, and he looked at her somewhat sheepishly, asking her not to rub it in, for he hadn't heard the alarm at all. He had slept through it, and not awakened Mrs. N. as promised.

However, the friendly ghost had seen to it that she didn't miss her morning train. Was it the same benign specter that had shielded them from the hostile Indians during their occupancy (that is, if the "dream" of Indians in war paint belonged to the past of the house, and was not merely an expression of a young girl's fancy)?

Ghosts have rarely harmed anyone except through fear on the part of the observer, of his own doing and because of his own ignorance about ghosts. In the few cases in which ghosts have attacked people, such as the ghostly abbot of Trondheim, it is simply a matter of mistaken identity, where extreme violence at the time of death has left a strong memory in the individual ghost. By and large, it is not dangerous to be a ghost hunter, or to witness phenomena of this kind.

8

Kirlian Photography and Psychic Photography— Hoax or Fact?

According to Dr. Thelma Moss of the Department of Clinical Medicine, UCLA at Los Angeles:

Kirlian [pronounced keer-lee-an] photography is actually pretty old. Electrical photography started about one hundred years ago and was considered an interesting curiosity. Nobody ever did very much about it until in the Soviet Union a man was able to learn something about living organisms—leaves, plants, people—by using an electrical current and pulsing it through an object because it showed such extraordinary things.

For example, a living leaf is quite green, but as it dies, all its luminescence goes. When photographing it repeatedly over two days, we see that it gradually fades away until we cannot photograph it anymore. It would be very easy for us to say, certainly when something is alive it has a lot more brilliance and luminescence than when it dies.

The question, of course, is, What is it we are looking at in Kirlian photography? We have mummies that we suspect are four thousand years old. As a layman I would expect a less brilliant emanation than from the hand of a living person. But taking a mummy's hand that is four thousand years old and applying the Kirlian effect to it and seeing it luminesce so brilliantly is mind-blowing. All I can say is this is a fascinating field to explore and maybe in ten years' time we will know what we are doing. Up to this moment in time, nobody knows.

Through Kirlian photography we've seen fascinating variations in people. You know, we tend to think of ourselves as living, emotional people that interact with other people in love and hate and so on. Though we think of this abstractly, there is such a thing as love and there is such a thing as hate. For example, when we get two loving people to put their hands quite close together, the emanations from the two are just intermingled with each other; whereas if they are registering something like antipathy or dislike for each other, the emanations literally repel each other, and sometimes brilliantly: you can see a barrier of light between them, as if there were something invisible cutting them off from one another.

These things are awfully difficult to explain in terms of conventional physics.

Dr. Moss told me that there are many different words used to describe this effect. Conventional physicists call it a corona discharge, which is an electrical emanation caused by the current and the voltage going through the object. People who are more inclined to the occult or to the mystical call it an aura. They compare it, for example, with famous paintings of saints or of Jesus—there are auras around the heads. These people believe that what we are photographing with this electrical photography is a representation of that, i.e., something invisible to the eye but existing in and around the body. People who are noncommittal, as I prefer to be, call it an emanation or some outpouring of energy. The Russians use a technical term to describe it—bioplasma.

People sometimes mistakenly assume that only living things, organic substances, give off these emanations. The fact is that coins, other metals—all kinds of strange things—give off emanations. It is interesting to note, however, that while inorganic objects like metals give a static emanation that never changes, the emanations of organic substances—a leaf or a person or an animal—are constantly, dynamically changing according to the way the animal or the plant is responding to its environment and to the people or objects that it comes in contact with.

These emanations are like frozen energy—energy that is still very much alive and emanating at various frequencies. As far as the emanations from a certain object are concerned, providing you are using the same instruments and the same electrical parameters, you will always get the same picture from a United States dime. However, if anyone put his finger on this coin, the picture on it would change dramatically, depending on whether the person was relaxed or anxious, or frightened, or even sexually aroused. All these things cause an almost instantaneous change. One of the most fascinating things we've found is called the dominance factor: If two people are photographed together with their fingers almost but not quite touching, and there is eye contact between them, one or the other person just disappears. This indicates to us that a person's vitality, or lifeforce, or energy, will change very much depending on how that person is reacting to another person. For example, when we photograph a family— father and mother and child—very often the child simply is not there. It is as if the father and mother somehow cause the child to disappear from the photograph.

Dr. Moss explained that there may be practical applications for this kind of photography:

> We are doing some preliminary work with cancerous and noncancerous rats. Cancerous rats show a visibly different pattern than do healthy rats without tumors. This has led to a more recent technique that detects heat changes in the body, which reveal areas of possible cancers. A series of experiments with the Orthopedic Hospital in Los Angeles has been planned. But only thousands of trials will decide the correlation between pictures.

The emanations do reveal certain kinds of information about communication between people. "We talk frequently about nonverbal communication," Dr. Moss explained. "I think if you look at emanations between people you will see that they are certainly communicating on a nonverbal level. Anger, antagonism, love, and other emotions are distinctly seen.

Anxiety, or fear, vividly shows as a violent red blotch in the photograph."

By comparing physical leaf emanations, diseases in plants can be detected before they manifest themselves. There seems to be something happening that is not physical but on the verge of becoming physical. However, work in this area shows that Kirlian photography has only just begun. Dr. Moss explained:

> We have all kinds of instrumentation and none of it has been standardized. All of the six instruments that we have in our various labs take different pictures. So each time we do something, if we take one leaf and we take six different pictures on six different instruments, we will get six different stories. What we need eventually is to be able to understand what the instruments are telling us, so that we can get repeatable effects whether the experiment is being done in the United States or in the Soviet Union or in Brazil. There are people all over the world who are working in this area. It is most encouraging to know that certain things are repeatable in different countries. The most dramatic finding that we have had is the "phantom leaf" effect. When we cut off a part of a leaf, we get the entire leaf revealed sometimes when we take its picture using the Kirlian technique. We have done it in our lab. It has been done in Brazil under Professor Andreade and it's also been done in Moscow. In other words, there seems to be a reliable and repeatable, if erratic, effect.

According to Dr. Moss, they have had various inquiries in their laboratory from some very strange sources.

> One of the sources that have come to speak to us is NASA, and their particular interest in Kirlian photography is very serious. If the Kirlian effect is a universal phenomenon, then living materials and dead materials can be photographically defined. NASA wanted to take one of these devices [Kirlian-photography instrument] on board their Mars probe. With television equipment the space scientists would be able to look

at microorganisms and by their luminescences see how or if they light up or if they resemble what we characteristically expect of living organisms on earth.

Kirlian photography got its start in Russia, when a group of scientists viewed the brilliant lights in a human body when it was placed in a field of high-frequency electrical currents. This demonstration was seen by Russia's foremost scientists and researchers from the prestigious Presidium of the Academy of Sciences of the USSR and from other leading institutes and universities in the Soviet Union. The group had discovered the strange powers of the human body.

The concept of a human aura—a radiating luminous cloud surrounding the body—goes back centuries. Pictures from early Egypt, India, Greece, and Rome show holy figures in a luminous surround long before artists in the Christian era began to paint the saints with halos. This practice may actually have been based on the observations of clairvoyants who reportedly could see the radiance surrounding saints. Mrs. Eileen Garrett, the famous psychic, reports in her book, *Awareness,* "I've always seen every plant, animal, and person encircled by a misty surround." According to people's moods, the surround changes color and consistency, she says.

Clairvoyants claim that *aura* is a misnomer; they believe that the human body is interpenetrated by another body of energy and it is the luminescence from the *second* body radiating outward that they see as the aura. We look, they say, something like a lunar eclipse of the sun, the luminous astral body being completely concealed by the physical body. Paracelsus, the philosopher, chemist, alchemist, and doctor, believed that a half-corporeal or "star" body lives in the flesh and is its mirror image.

In the early 1900s, Dr. Walter Kilner of St. Thomas' Hospital in London discovered that by looking through glass screens stained with dicyanine dye, he could actually see the aura around the human body. According to Dr. Kilner, it was a cloud of radiation extending out about six to eight inches and showing distinct colors. Disease, fatigue, or mood could alter the size and color; this radiation was also affected by magnetism, electricity, and hypnosis. He developed an entire system for diagnosing illness from the aura, and research on the aura is continuing in Europe.

The first hint that there was more to the human body than had previously been thought by Russian scientists began back in 1939 in Krasnodar Krai, the capital city of the Kuban region in the south of Russia near the Black Sea. "Where can I get technical equipment repaired?" a research scientist asked a colleague. Soviets at research institutes, labs, and various businesses all agreed: "Go to Semyon Davidovich Kirlian, if you want a repair done properly. He's the best electrician in Krasnodar."

Kirlian was called. While picking up the equipment at the research institute, Kirlian chanced to see a demonstration of a high-frequency instrument for electrotherapy. As the patient received treatment through the electrodes of the machine, Kirlian suddenly noticed a tiny flash of light between the electrodes and the patient's skin. "I wonder if I could photograph that," he mused. "What if I put a photographic plate between the patient's skin and the electrodes?"

But the electrodes were made of glass and the photoplate would be spoiled by exposure to light before the machine could be switched on. He would have to use a metal electrode, which would be dangerous. He considered this a sacrifice for science, and attached the metal electrode to his own hand.

As he switched on the machine, Kirlian felt a stabbing pain in his hand under the metal electrode. It was a severe burn. Three seconds later, the machine was switched off and Kirlian rushed the photoplate into the emulsion. As the picture developed he could make out a strange imprint on it, a kind of luminescence in the shape of the contours of his fingers. "I studied the picture with pain, excitement and hope all combined," said Kirlian. "Did I have a discovery? An invention? It wasn't clear yet."

He discovered that scientists had observed this phenomenon before, but the information had been filed in their research reports and forgotten. He followed his hunch and soon his esteemed talent and ingenuity at electronics were at work on this new project. Other techniques of photographing without light—X-ray, infrared, radioactivity—were of no help. He therefore had to devise a whole new process to record on film the luminous energy coming from the human body. And so, with his wife, Valentina, a teacher and journalist, Kirlian invented an entirely new method of photography, which holds some fourteen patents.

But the photographs showed only static images. Soon the Kirlians developed a special optical instrument so that they could directly observe the phenomenon in motion. Kirlian held his hand under the lens and switched on the current. And then a fantastic world of the unseen opened before them.

The hand itself looked like the Milky Way in a starry sky. Against a background of blue and gold, something was taking place in his hand that looked like a fireworks display. Multicolored flares lit up, then sparks, twinkles, flashes. Some lights glowed steadily like Roman candles; others flashed out, then dimmed. Still others sparkled at intervals. In parts of his hand were little dim clouds. Certain glittering flares meandered along sparkling labyrinths like spaceships traveling to other galaxies.

The investigators examined under their high-frequency microscope every conceivable substance—leather, metal, wood, rubber, paper, coins, leaves. The pattern of luminescence was different for every item, but living things had totally different structural details from nonliving things. A metal coin, for instance, showed only a completely even glow all around the edges. But a living leaf was made up of millions of sparkling lights that glowed and glittered like jewels. The flares along its edges were individual and different from one another.

Soon many great Soviet scientists traveled to Krasnodar Krai. There were the famous and the curious. There were members of the Academy of Science as well as ministers of the government. Over some thirteen years, there were hundreds of visitors. Doctors, biophysicists, biochemists, electronics experts, criminology specialists—all appeared at the door of the little one-story, prerevolutionary wooden house on Kirov Street in Krasnodar.

The philosophical implications were even more extraordinary. It seemed that living things had two bodies: the physical body that everyone could see, and a secondary "energy body," which the Kirlians saw in their high-frequency photos. The energy body didn't seem to be only a radiation of the physical body. The physical body appeared to *mirror* what was happening in the energy body. If an imbalance in this energy body of the plant occurred, it indicated illness, and gradually the physical body would reflect this change. Would this be true of human beings too? they wondered. Fatigue, illness, states of mind, thoughts, emotion, all make their distinctive imprint on the pattern of energy that seems to circulate continuously through the human body.

Medical professors such as Dr. S. M. Pavlenko, chairman of the Pathology-Physiology Department of the First Moscow Medical Institute, reported, "Kirlian photography can be used for early diagnosis of disease, especially of cancer."

Sheila Ostrander and Lynn Schroeder, in their monumental work *Psychic Discoveries Behind the Iron Curtain,* summed up the Kirlians' contribution to science:

> Semyon Davidovich Kirlian and Valentina Chrisanfovna Kirlian had created a way for us to see the unseeable. But what did it mean—this maze of colored energy within us? Now they set the world of Soviet science on the track of some truly awesome discoveries about the nature of man. The Kirlians' "window on the Unknown" might revolutionize our entire concept of ourselves and our universe. It seems they had discovered far more than the aura.

For the past one hundred years, psychic research has continued to gather proof of the continuance of life and has gradually gone from the metaphysical world into the full glare of scientific inquiry. Although sometimes interpreted according to personal attitudes, it is no longer possible to bury the evidence itself, as some materialistically inclined scientists in other fields have attempted to do over the years. The challenge is always present: does man have a soul, scientifically speaking, and if so, how can we prove it?

There is a great deal of material on communications with the so-called dead. But additional proof that man does continue an existence in what Dr. Joseph Rhine has called "the world of the mind" was always wanted, especially the kind of proof that could be viewed objectively, without need for subjective observation through psychic experiences, either spontaneous or induced in the laboratory. One of the greatest potential tools was given to man when photography was invented: for if we could photograph the dead under conditions that carefully exclude trickery, we would surely be much the wiser—and the argument for survival after physical death would indeed be stronger.

Photography itself goes back to the 1840s, when the technique evolved gradually from very crude light-and-shadow pictures, through daguerreotypes and tintypes, to photography as we now know it.

Major Tom Patterson, a British psychic researcher, in a recent booklet entitled "Spirit Photography," has dealt with the beginnings of photographic mediumship in Britain, where it has produced the largest amount of experimental material in the century since photography began.

But the initial experiment took place in 1862, in Boston, not Britain, twenty-three years after photography itself came into being. William H. Mumler, an engraver, who was neither interested in nor a believer in Spiritualism, or any other form of psychic research, had been busy in his off hours experimenting with a camera. At that time, photographic cameras were still a novelty. The engraver liked to take snapshots of his family and friends to learn more about his camera. Imagine Mr. Mumler's surprise and dismay when some of his negatives showed faces that were not supposed to be on them. Alongside the "formal" portraits of the living people Mumler had so carefully posed and photographed were portraits of their dead relatives.

To obtain any sort of images on photographic paper, especially recognizable pictures such as faces or figures, without having first made a negative in the usual manner, is, of course, scientifically impossible—*except* in psychic photography.

Until the invention of Polaroid cameras and Polaroid film, this was certainly one-hundred-percent true. The Polaroid method, with its almost instant development process, adds to experiments the valuable element of close supervision. It allows an even more direct contact between psychic radiation and sensitive surface. The disadvantage of Polaroid photography is its ephemeral character. Even the improved film does not promise to stay unspoiled forever, and it is wise to protect unusual Polaroid photographs by obtaining slide copies. Actually, Polaroid photography uses a combination of film and sensitive paper simultaneously, one being peeled off the other after the instant development process inside the camera.

Fakery with the ordinary type of photography would depend on double exposure or double printing by unscrupulous operators, in which case no authentic negative could be produced that would stand up to *experienced* scrutiny. Fakery with Polaroid equipment is impossible if camera, film, and operator are closely watched. Because of the great light sensitivity of Polaroid film, double exposure, if intended, is not a simple matter, as one exposure would severely cancel out the other and certainly leave traces of double exposure. And the film, of course, would have to be switched in the presence of the observer, something not even a trained conjurer is likely to do to an experienced psychic investigator. A psychic researcher, in order to qualify for the title, must be familiar with magic and sleight-of-hand tricks.

The important thing to remember about psychic photography is that the bulk of it occurs unexpectedly and often embarrassingly to amateur photographers not the least bit interested in parapsychology or any form of occultism. The "extras" on the negatives were not placed there by these photographers or their subjects to confuse *themselves.* The literature on this aspect of psychic photography, notably in Britain, is impressive; and I particularly recommend the scholarly work by F. W. Warrick, the celebrated British parapsychologist, called *Experiments in Psychics,* in which hundreds of experimental photographs have been reproduced. Mr. Warrick's work concerns itself primarily with the photographic mediumship of Mrs. Emma Deane, although other examples are included. It was published in 1939 by E. P. Dutton. Mr. Warrick points out that he and his colleagues, having spent some thirty years working with and closely supervising their subjects, knew their personal habits and quirks. Any kind of trickery was therefore out of the question, unless one wanted to call a researcher who propounded unusual ideas self-deluded or incompetent, as some latter-day critics have done to Harry Price and Sir William Crookes, respected British psychic researchers, now dead.

In England, the craft of psychic photography developed slowly after the 1870s. The first man in Britain to show successful results in this field was Frederick Hudson, who in 1872 produced a number of authentic likenesses of the dead taken under conditions excluding fraud. Several experiments were performed under the careful scrutiny of Dr. Alfred Russel Wallace, who attested to the genuineness of the observed phenomena. Since then, several dozen talented psychic photographers have appeared on the scene, producing *for a few pennies* genuine likenesses of persons known to have died previously in the presence of "sitters" (or portrait subjects) they had never before met in their lives.

Often, psychic photography occurs at so-called home circles, where neither money nor notoriety is involved and where, certainly, those taking the pictures have no need for self-delusion. They are, presumably, already convinced of survival of personality after death, otherwise they would not be members of the circle.

Photographs of ghosts or haunted areas are much

rarer because of the great element of chance in obtaining any results at all. Whereas psychic photography in the experimental sense is subject to schedules and human plans, the taking of ghost pictures is not.

We still don't know *all* the conditions that make these extraordinary photographs possible, and, until we do, obtaining them will be a hit-and-miss affair at best. But the fact that genuine photographs of what are commonly called ghosts have been taken by a number of people, under conditions excluding fraud or faulty equipment, is of course food for serious thought.

The latest development in the area of psychic photography, although not concerned with images of ghosts, is still germane to the issue. Thought forms registering on photographic film or other light-sensitive surfaces are the result of years of hard work by Colorado University's Professor Jule Eisenbud, a well-known psychiatrist interested in parapsychology as well, with Chicago photographic medium Ted Serios. These amazing pictures have recently been published by Eisenbud in an impressive volume called *The World of Ted Serios*. (Serios has the uncanny ability of projecting onto film or TV tubes images of objects and scenes often at great distances in space, or even *time*. This includes places he has never seen before.) In addition, more material becomes available as the experiments continue, thanks to the efforts of a number of universities and study groups who have belatedly recognized the importance of psychic photography and related subjects.

9
Criminal Detection Work and ESP

It is entirely possible that extrasensory perception has great practical value in crime detection. In fact, law enforcement agencies are using it more and more often. This does not mean that the courts will openly admit evidence obtained by psychic means. However, it does mean that a psychic may help the authorities solve a crime by leading them to a criminal or missing person—it is then up to the police or other agency to establish the facts by *conventional* means that will stand up in a court of law.

One of the most talented psychics who helped police and the FBI was the late Florence Sternfels, who was also a great psychometrist. She would pick up a trail from such meager clues as an object belonging to the criminal or missing person, or even merely by being asked what had happened to the person. Of course, she had no access to any information about the cases she helped with, nor was she ever told afterward how the cases ended. Police and other law enforcement agencies like to come to psychics for help, but once they've gotten what they came for, they are reluctant to keep the psychics informed of progress they have made as a result of the leads provided. They are even more reluctant to admit that a psychic has helped them. This can take on preposterous proportions.

The Dutch psychic Peter Hurkos, whose help was sought by the Boston police, was able to describe in great detail the killer in the case under investigation:

that of the Boston Strangler. Hurkos, who had come to Boston to help the authorities, soon found himself in the middle of a power play between the Boston police and the Massachusetts attorney general. The police has close ties to Boston's Democratic machine, and the attorney general was a Republican. Hurkos, even worse, was a foreigner.

When the newspapers splashed over their front pages the psychic's successful tracing of the killer, something within the police department snapped. Hurkos, certain that he had picked the right suspect, returned to New York, his job done. The following morning he was arrested on the charge of impersonating an FBI man several months before; he had allegedly said as much to a gas station attendant and shown him some credentials. This happened when the gas station man noticed some rifles in Hurkos's car. The "credentials" were honorary police cards that many grateful police chiefs had given the psychic for his aid. Hurkos, whose English was fragmentary, said something to the effect that he worked with the FBI, which was perfectly true. To a foreigner, the difference between such a statement and an assertion of being an FBI man is negligible and perhaps unimportant.

Those in the know realized that Hurkos was being framed, and some papers said so immediately. Then the attorney general's office picked up another suspect, who practically matched the first one's appearance, weight, height, and even profession—that of a shoe salesman. Which salesman did the killing? But Hurkos had done his job well. He had pointed out the places where victims had been found and he had described the killer. And what did it bring him for his troubles, beyond a modest fee of one thousand dollars? Only trouble and embarrassment.

Florence Sternfels was more fortunate in her police contacts. During the early part of World War II, she strongly felt that the Iona Island powder depot would be blown up by saboteurs. She had trouble getting to the right person, of course, but eventually she succeeded, and the detonation was headed off just in the nick of time. I learned that Professor Holzer had known and sometimes worked with Ms. Sternfels, and he claims that she was consulted in dozens of cases of mysterious disappearance of persons. He told me that in one instance she was flown to Colorado to help local authorities track down a murderer. Never frightened, she saw the man captured a day or two later.

Incidentally, she never charged a penny for her work with law enforcement agencies.

The well-known Dutch clairvoyant Gerard Croiset has worked with the police on a number of cases of murder and disappearance. In the United States, Croiset attempted to solve the almost legendary disappearance of Judge Crater, with the help of his biographer, Jack Harrison Pollack. Although Pollack succeeded in adding new material, he was not able to actually find the bones in the spot indicated by him clairvoyantly. However, Croiset was of considerable help in the case of three murdered civil-rights workers. He supplied, again through Jack Pollack, a number of clues and pieces of information as to where the bodies would be found, who the murderers were, and how the crime had been committed, at a time when even the question of whether they were dead had not yet been resolved!

Croiset "sees" in pictures rather than in words or sentences. He need not be present at the scene of a crime to get impressions, but it helps him to hold an object belonging to the person whose fate he is to fathom.

At least some police officers do not hesitate to speak up, and openly admit the importance of ESP in their work. An interview with Lieutenant John J. Cronin was published in the New York *Journal-American* on October 9, 1964.

"In the not too distant future, every police department in the land will have extra-sensory perception consultants, perhaps even extra-sensory perception bureaus," New York Police Lt. John J. Cornin said today.

For 18 years—longer than any other man in the history of the department—he headed the Missing Persons Bureau.

"After I retire, I might write a book on ESP," he said. "It has provided much information on police cases that is accurate."

One of the fantastic cases he cited was that of a 10-year-old Baltimore girl who was missing last July.

A Baltimore sergeant visited Mrs. Florence Sternfels of Edgewater, New Jersey, who calls herself a psychometrist. On her advice, when he got back to Baltimore he dug in a neighbor's cellar. The body of the girl was found two feet under the dirt floor.

More specific about the methods used by psychics in helping solve crimes is a column written by Michael MacDougall for the *Long Island Press*, May 3, 1964, in which he suggested that people with ESP powers should be on the staff of every police department to help solve difficult crimes. Columnist MacDougall made a very strong case for his convictions when he wrote up the following incident, which took place a month earlier, on Friday, April 3, involving DeMille, the famous mentalist.

DeMille, on a lecture tour for the Associated Executives Clubs, checked into the Chinook Hotel in Yakima Wash., at 2 P.M. He was tired, intended to shower and sleep before that evening's speech at the Knife and Fork Club. But he had hardly turned the key in the lock when the telephone rang.

It was a woman calling to tell him that her friend had had her wallet stolen. She then asked him if he could help them recover some of the articles of sentimental value contained in it.

"Perhaps," said DeMille. "I'll do my best. But you'll have to wait until after my speech. Call me about 10:30."

DeMille hung up, tumbled into bed. But he couldn't sleep. The thought of that stolen wallet intruded. Then, just on the edge of unconsciousness, when one is neither asleep nor awake, he envisioned the crime.

Two teenaged boys, one wearing a red sweater, stole up behind a woman shopper. One stepped in front, diverting her attention, while the other gently unfastened her handbag, removed her wallet, went around the corner, and waited to be joined later by his partner.

Next, DeMille saw the two boys get into a beat-up Ford. They drove away, parked briefly in front of a used-car lot. Opening the wallet, they took out a roll of bills, which were divided evenly. DeMille wasn't sure of the count but thought it was $46. Then the boys examined a checkbook. DeMille saw the number 2798301, and the legend: First National Bank of Washington. He also received an impression that it was some kind of a meat-packing firm.

Now fully awake, DeMille phoned K. Gordon Smith, secretary of the Knife and Fork Club. The secretary came up to DeMille's room, listened to the story, and advised calling the police.

Again, DeMille told his story to Sergeant Walt Dutcher, of the Yakima Police, and Frank Gayman, a reporter for the *Yakima Herald*. The sergeant was totally disbelieving and openly hostile. Gayman was skeptical but willing to be convinced.

DeMille suggested they call the First National Bank and find out if a meat-packing company had a checking account numbered 2798301. Then, perhaps, they could verify at least part of the story for the police.

The report was negative. Account #2798301 was not a meat-packing company. In fact, the bank had no meat packers as customers. Fruit packers, yes; meat packers, no.

Sergeant Dutcher, after threatening DeMille with arrest for turning in a false crime report, stamped out of the room. Frank Gayman, still willing to be convinced, remained. The phone rang again. It was for Gayman; the bank was calling.

There was an account numbered 2798001 carried by Cub Scout Pack #3. Could this be the one? Immediately, DeMille knew that it was.

The President of the Knife and Fork Club, Karl Steinhilb, volunteered to drive DeMille about the city. Following the mentalist's directions, Steinhilb drove to an outlying section, parked in front of a used-car lot. And sure enough, in the bushes fronting a nearby house they found the discarded wallet.

Far and away the most intriguing use of psychic detectives in real police work occurred in St. Louis. Thanks to Detective John Kiriakos, I was able to learn the story of the Lucas case in which the work of a psychic was most effective.

I arrived in St. Louis more curious than anything else. Over the course of the last year I had read fleeting newspaper accounts of Bevy Jaegers and her Psychic Rescue Squad who use their powers of ESP to solve crimes and locate missing persons. The articles were sprinkled with quotes by the local police who freely admitted they had worked with Bevy and that she had an uncanny ability to come up with clues long after they had exhausted every possible lead. Such brash statements coming from closed-mouthed law enforcement officials peaked my interest, and prompted me to delve deeper into the world of psychic detection.

In my years of filmmaking, I had read countless detective stories in search of good script material. I felt that I was an expert on the methodology of every classical detective. I wondered how different the approach of psychic Bevy Jaegers would be from the analytical genius of Sherlock Holmes, or the cynical determination of Phillip Marlowe. Was ESP just another name for the finely tuned intuition of these fictional detectives?

I took the Red Eye from Los Angeles and arrived in St. Louis in time for breakfast. Bevy had made me promise that I'd come straight from the airport. At 8:30 A.M. on an icy November morning I found myself on the doorstep of a typical suburban home, being welcomed by a not-so-typical housewife.

Bevy is an imposing woman. As we stood face to face I was mesmerized by her look. I felt as if her eyes could read every thought in my mind.

Before Bevy would give me the details of the Lucas case, she insisted on laying down some basic groundwork so that I would understand *her* notion of ESP. "ESP," she said, "is an extension of our normal awareness that goes far beyond what's considered ordinary or natural. It used to be considered supernatural, but it can't be because everybody has it. It's just a matter of developing it." She told me that over the course of ten years she had helped sixteen people in the St. Louis area develop their psychic abilities.

Members of her Psychic Detective Squad hold down normal, nine to five jobs. They come together for weekly training sessions and to work on special cases. Bevy compared the routine of the psychic detective to an athlete in training. She told me that we have to exercise our psychic muscles to keep them in shape. It's a matter of a special form of "mind stretching" that allows us to tap our psychic energy.

According to Bevy, each member of the squad brings his own specialty to the art of solving crimes. Some people psychically tune-in to the location of a crime, others feel a connection with the victim, while some can pick up on the motives of the perpetrator. The collective information supplied by squad members is fitted together like a vast jig-saw puzzle before Bevy goes to the police with their impressions.

Bevy then related the story of how it all began. Her interest in ESP had caused her to set up a weekly workshop for anyone who wanted to explore their own psychic potential. In 1971, a case of a missing person came into the headlines and stayed there for weeks because of the bizarre circumstances that surrounded it. The case, which came to be known as the Lucas case, aroused Bevy's interest. It seems that a St. Louis socialite named Sally Lucas had disappeared from a suburban shopping center. The police could find no reason for her disappearance, and no clues to her whereabouts.

Members of the ESP class felt that this was an opportunity to use the skills they had been developing towards a practical end. What they needed to begin the process of psychic crime detection was something belonging to the missing woman. A close family friend supplied Bevy with a nightgown and a powder-puff. From holding these two items, Bevy received some strong psychic impressions that she wrote down and sent to a well-known crime reporter on the St. Louis *Globe Democrat*. Bill Fuestel, a crusty journalist who has been with the *Globe Democrat* for twenty years, was stunned by the accuracy of Bevy's first impressions.

When I interviewed Fuestel in his smokey cubbyhole at the *Globe Democrat,* he told me that his first reaction was that somehow Bevy had access to confidential information. He said that her random impressions contained facts about Sally Lucas's private life that the police were not letting out. But the thing that convinced Fuestel that Bevy should be brought into the case did not happen until the next day. Bevy had told Bill Fuestel that she "saw" Sally Lucas's car near a large body of water that she thought was the ocean. The car was abandoned, and Bevy said that a group of police were surrounding it. The next morning the car was discovered by the police in Florida, no more than fifty feet from the Gulf of Mexico.

Fuestel then made the decision to approach a St. Louis police detective, John Kiriakos, widely known for his ability to crack tough cases. By that time, Kiriakos had exhausted all of his leads in the Lucas case, and just might be receptive to Fuestel's unorthodox scheme.

Fuestel called Kiriakos and said, "I want to do something unusual. I want to bring a psychic down to headquarters and let her sit in Sally Lucas's car and see what kind of impressions she gets." Fuestel reports that at first "John laughed at me and said to stop putting him on." But Fuestel didn't let up, and the detective finally relented.

Lt. John Kiriakos remembers the incident well. As a hard-nosed detective with twenty-three years on the force, he relies on clues, evidence and informants to solve criminal investigations. But with nothing whatsoever to go on, he was willing to consider Bill Fuestel's crazy scheme.

The next morning Bevy, her husband Ray, and one member of the squad appeared at the police station. Bevy was allowed to sit in the Lucas car and gather her psychic impressions. The way that Fuestel and Kiriakos describe it, she held on to the steering wheel and closed her eyes. After a few minutes of deep concentration, she began to jot down her perceptions on paper. Fuestel still has the loose-leaf sheets that are covered with Bevy's scrawl. He showed them to me, and in light of the story I was about to hear, they are the best concrete evidence I have seen yet that information can be transmitted by an unknown energy force, in unknown ways.

Bevy had seen what she describes as a "motion picture" flicker through her mind's eye. She had seen Sally Lucas driving out of the shopping center parking lot with a young man seated next to her. The unknown man forced Mrs. Lucas to drive to a wooded area on the outskirts of St. Louis. Bevy describes the area as follows, "I saw horses and the letter 'C.' I didn't know what 'C' meant, but it kept coming back to me. Then I was sitting in Sally Lucas's place at the wheel and we were driving down a country road. I saw a row of pillar-like mailboxes, and then there was a shallow creek and a white bridge over it. For some reason the word 'poker' kept flashing through my mind, but that didn't seem to fit at all."

Then came what Bevy describes as the most intense psychic experience of her life. As she was sitting in the car she felt as though she had assumed Sally Lucas's identity. She felt a crushing blow to the right side of her head and severe physical pain. Fuestel remembers the moment when the pain hit. He says that "Bevy looked like she was in real agony. She wasn't acting." Bevy herself told me that the experience was so real that she had to break her trance and get out of the car.

Bevy, her husband Ray, and psychic squad member Jim Mueller decided that they would follow Bevy's impressions and go out into the field. Bevy associated the wooded area that she had "seen" in her trance with Babler State Park, a sprawling game preserve about forty miles southwest of the city. The three detectives spent the next four hours combing the park until they arrived at a particularly dense area known as Wild Horse Creek. Suddenly Bevy felt what she describes as a "magnetic needle" swinging inside her. It pointed in a specific direction, and she felt certain that her psychic sense was correct. Ray and Jim followed Bevy's lead through the underbrush of Wild Horse Creek. They noted that the last road they turned off of was

Highway "C" just at the point where it crossed Highway "CC."

As the hunt for Sally Lucas continued, Bevy found herself pulled towards a shallow creek. By the time she saw a small white bridge that crossed over the creek, her internal compass was swinging wildly. But the light was beginning to fade, and Bevy, Ray and Jim realized that they would have to continue their investigation the next day.

The next morning a rain storm drenched St. Louis. The three waited inside impatiently for two days, hoping that the weather would clear. The morning that the rain stopped, Sally Lucas's decomposed body was discovered no more that thirty feet away from the creek that Bevy had searched two days earlier. The heavy rain had washed her body out of the thick underbrush.

As Lt. Kiriakos tells it, the realization that Bevy had been amazingly accurate didn't sink in until hours after the body had been found. As he was reliving the day's events for his wife, he suddenly realized that all of Bevy's clues had been correct. The horse, the letter "C," and even the word "Poker" which stood for a near-by farm called "Poker Flats" were right on the mark. But above all, Bevy's impression that Sally Lucas had been killed by a blow to the right side of the head was corroborated by the autopsy report, which indicated that a heavy object was used to crush her skull.

The pin-point accuracy of Bevy's impressions encouraged her to forge ahead with her work as a psychic detective. Since the Lucas case, she has found it necessary to establish the squad as a licensed detective bureau. Only with a detective's license is Bevy permitted to submit evidence to a court of law.

She has also made a rule for herself that the squad will only accept case referrals from the police. This insures that the squad will be working in complete harmony with the police on all cases. Also, Bevy does not publicize any of the cases the squad takes on because she is afraid that if the squad's identity is known the members may be exposed to physical harm by a criminal who is still at large.

Bevy hopes to be able to prove to law enforcement officials that her kind of detective work can be useful. Eventually she would like to be able to train police to develop their own psychic gifts, and I have the feeling that she might even be able to teach Sherlock Holmes and Phillip Marlowe a thing or two.

One of the schools that specialize in work with clairvoyants who cooperate with police is the University of Utrecht, Netherlands, where Dr. W. H. C. Tenhaeff is the head of the Parapsychology Institute. Between 1950 and 1960 alone, over forty psychics were studied by the institute, including twenty-six men and twenty-one women, according to author-researcher Jack Harrison Pollack, who visited the institute in 1960 and wrote a glowing report on its activities.

The University of Utrecht is, in this respect, far ahead of the other schools. In the United States, Dr. Joseph B. Rhine made a brilliant initial effort, but today Duke University's parapsychology laboratory is doing little to advance the research in ESP beyond repeat experiments and very cautious theorizing on the nature of man. There is practically no field work being done outside the laboratory, and no American university is in a position, either financially or staff-wise, to investigate a work with such brilliant psychics as does Dr. Tenhaeff in Holland.

10
Psychic Surgery and Healing

One of the most controversial subjects in the field of parapsychology, I discovered, is psychic surgery—opinions go all the way from cries of outright fraud to complete belief. So far, nobody has made a completely foolproof investigation to determine the full truth, but I am convinced, from my own research, that the truth lies somewhere in the middle. Certainly, the evidence of cases of genuine psychic surgery is strong.

Actually, Brazilian psychic surgeons preceded those at the Philippine clinics by several years. Brazil, which has a large Spiritualist population, has always taken a more progressive approach to "unorthodox" healing. According to John Frances-Phipps, and the *Psychic News* of November 29, 1969, there are hundreds of psychic surgeons in Brazil. In a series of articles, Frances-Phipps described in vivid language his personal experiences with the healers Lourival de Freitas and the late Jose Arigo.

The late Jose Arigo saw thousands of patients at his clinic in Congohas Do Compo. Arigo's guide, Dr. Fritz, was a spirit doctor, who spoke with a marked German accent or in German, which Arigo did not understand. Through the entranced Dr. Fritz, Arigo would prescribe various medicines and treatments for his patients. In some ways the approach resembled that of the late Edgar Cayce. Dr. Andrija Puharich, who spent much time with the late Arigo, is fully convinced of the genuineness of the phenomenon; he himself had a growth removed from his arm by the spirit healer.

Arigo was killed in an auto accident at a time when he finally was getting recognition and protection from a jealous medical establishment that had attempted to jail him several times, and when a special hospital of 160 beds was being built in his honor and for his use. But he, the Brazilian psychic surgeons, the Philippines' Tony Agpaoa, and others less well known, who practice along similar lines, are by no means isolated cases.

Thus, in 1967 a British medium and healer, Isa Northage, performed psychic surgery on Scottish bus driver Tommy Hanlon, who suffered from a stomach ulcer. The surgery was witnessed by Hanlon's aunt, a registered nurse named Margaret Sim. Miss Sim closely observed the healer's work. To begin with, the healer massaged the patient's abdomen. Then, before the witness's astonished eyes, Hanlon's stomach wall was opened up—in her words, "opened like a rose"—and the ulcer was taken out in two pieces, with forceps. The healer then closed the wound. There was no trace of a scar. According to a reporter for the *Psychic News,* Hanlon was able to eat normally an hour after the operation.

Isa Northage, of Nottingham, works with a spirit doctor by the name of Dr. Reynolds. Photographs of malignancies were offered in evidence of another successful psychic surgery by Mrs. Northage. These malignancies came from the jaw of Mrs. Sylvia Hudstone, who signed a testimonial to the effect that she was cured completely by Mrs. Northage. During the operation, the patient felt no pain whatever, and the entire proceedings took place in front of a large audience in Mrs. Northage's Spiritualist church at Pinewoods, Nottingham.

Harold Sherman, the "grand old man of psychics," investigated the Philippino "wonder healers," as he calls them, in person. Sherman quoted Philippino investigator Ulpiano Guiang, a lawyer by profession, concerning the most prominent of the Philippino surgeons, Tony Agpaoa:

"As of now, I would evaluate Tony's healings as definitely divine in nature. His towering, bare-hand surgical performances are, in my opinion, above the knowledge and skill of professional medical practitioners. Tony moves freely, modestly, without any extraordinary physical culture; no special skill in any field of athletic or mechanical know-how. He knows little of medical terms, and has had no training, except the experience that has come to him through functioning of this divine power.

"Jealousy of Tony and his work is inevitable. He lives under the threat of being arrested for violation of medical practice at any time, despite the great following that he now has. Yet, I am continuing my investigations as best I can to find out more and more of the truth about Tony's healings.

"I saw a heart operation on Mrs. Angela Villarino of Tondo, Manila, but I did not fully describe it because there were dual operations on the liver and heart. I did not explain in detail how he got through the rib cage. On the next operation on a heart, a sister of Mrs. Villarino's of 2604 Juan Luna, Tondo, Manila, I will make a full history and give you detailed information on the operations. The heart operation to be performed will be accompanied by two relative physicians as arranged by Mrs. Villarino, as soon as Tony comes home from Bukidnon, Mandanao, perhaps before the end of this month."

Charges of fraud persisted, however, against Tony and the several lesser-known Philippino psychic surgeons. B. S. Sharma, a Spiritualist from Delhi, India, observed Philippino psychic surgeons at work in Manila. Sharma claimed that the material taken from the bodies of the patients was in fact "a waxy substance dexterously palmed and skillfully twisted to make it appear as if it is drawn out of the patient's body." However, a team of would-be investigators visited Tony Agpaoa to obtain this body tissue and had it examined in a laboratory. The tissue was then declared, on the opinion of one medical researcher, to be of animal origin, and, again on the testimony of one researcher, the entire field of psychic surgery was called fraudulent and the "wonder healers of the Philippines" were referred to as charlatans and frauds.

There is much confusion concerning healing: what it represents, and what comes under the heading of healing and what does not. Many people think that all healing is a matter of belief and suggestion. Nothing could be further from the truth. Unorthodox healing —that is, healing procedures that are contrary to current medical thinking—includes a number of approaches.

First, there is *psychic healing*. This is a form of *mediumship* in which the healer draws psychic energy from himself, principally from the solar plexus area and the top of the head, and through his hands places this energy on the body of the patient, particularly on the areas in which he has seen or felt the presence of illness. Diagnosis always precedes healing. Psychic healers are able to look at a person and see discolorations in the person's aura or magnetic field. They will then tune in on that area. The psychic healer rarely touches the skin of his patient. His healing takes place at the periphery of the personality where the aura ends and where it is therefore more sensitive, just as nerve endings are more sensitive than the middle parts of nerve tissue.

Psychic healing takes place whether or not the patient believes in it, in fact whether or not the healer himself believes in it. The ability to draw certain energies from the personality and apply them where they are needed is purely mechanistic. The ability to be a psychic healer has nothing to do with the healer's religious beliefs. Some psychic healers are Spiritualists and prefer to ascribe their abilities to the intervention of spirit entities, but the fact seems to be that the results are the same whether the healer is a Spiritualist or merely someone possessing extraordinary healing powers.

Physical healers are those who touch the body of the patient and apply a combination of psychic energy and directional massage, similar to the magnetic strokes of Dr. Mesmer, the father of modern hypnosis. The physical healer may or may not manipulate the body of his subject, and his healing is due primarily to the *laying on of hands,* through which the process of healing takes place. When a priest or, in rare cases, a layman places his hands on a patient, in order to heal him, physical healing is involved even though the process may contain spiritual overtones.

I discovered that one of the most successful psychic healers is a modest Georgia housewife by the name of Betty Dye. She is the mother of several children, the wife of a slight, soft-spoken man who works for one of the major oil companies, and a medium. Not just a woman with a prophetic vision of the world to come— and a fine record of past predictions come true—Betty Dye has the power of spiritual healing, and has worked with and been tested by Professor Hans Holzer. She comes from a devout Southern Baptist background and believes that the power to heal stems directly from God.

James Douglas DePass of Atlanta, who is an author and an officer of the Atlanta Theosophical Society, consulted Betty Dye in December 1970. In response, Mrs. Dye went into a trance, during which one of her controls, who identified himself as a doctor in physical life, diagnosed Mr. DePass's ailment as being connected with the stomach. Mrs. Dye had not been told anything about her visitor's problem. The entranced medium then laid her hands on the affected areas of the patient. Mr. DePass's pains left him by the end of the first sitting. During the trance, Mrs. Dye felt completely unattached to the proceedings and at one time grew very dizzy.

James DePass signed a notarized affidavit stating:

This is to acknowledge and certify that on a Sunday night in December 1970, Betty Dye with her spiritual healing talent did absolutely beyond doubt heal me of a stomach ailment. I had suffered nausea and stomach pain for a week. I had definitely decided to see my medical doctor the next day. No one knew of my trouble except my wife Hazel. It was an absolutely effective spiritual healing case administered by Betty Dye for which I am very grateful.

For thirty years the work of the late John Myers has been respected in psychical-research circles and somewhat controversially in scientifically oriented and lay circles. The respect was due John Myers, who passed away in May 1972, because of his unusual contributions to the fields of psychic photography and psychic healing.

The cases Myers cured number several hundred; they are on record. But perhaps the most outstanding of his cases was also his first really important one: Myers's meeting with American business executive R. L. Parish, who was then suffering from a chronic sciatic condition as well as from defective vision. Within a few days after Myers's treatment, the pain from the sciatic nerve ceased and for the first time in many years Parish was able to see without glasses.

Interestingly, Myers was even able to heal himself, something very few psychic healers can do. In 1957 he suffered a serious hemorrhage and in the middle of the night was taken to Medical Arts Hospital in New York City. His personal physician, Dr. Karl Fischbach, examined him and discovered a growth over the right kidney. Several cancer experts examined Myers subsequently, and biopsies were taken in the operating room to determine whether the growth was malignant. The unanimous verdict was that an immediate operation was imperative, that any delay might prove fatal.

John Myers steadfastly refused. He informed his doctors that he had no intention of being operated upon but would do for himself what he had often done for others. Myers remained in the hospital for one week for observation. During that time he healed himself, calling upon the divine powers that had helped him so many times before. His cancer disappeared at the end of the week, never to return.

I discovered that the venerable Los Angeles psychic Lotte von Strahl is now working as a psychic healer. Although she sees people at her studio in Westwood, all healing work she does is performed in the presence of or after consultation with a medical doctor. Mrs. von Strahl began her career as a psychic healer in

South Africa during World War II when a leading South African surgeon asked her to try to help his mother, who was suffering from blindness in one eye and partial blindness in the other. Mrs. von Strahl placed her hands upon the old woman, who reported immediate relief. Altogether, twelve sittings were necessary to accomplish what was asked of Mrs. Von Strahl. After that, the woman was able to read and even knit.

About the same time, another patient came to her, because the medical doctors had dismissed him as a hopeless case. After he had fallen from a ladder, a tumor had formed at the base of his spine. Mrs. von Strahl started to treat him by placing her hands upon the spot where she psychically saw the tumor. At the same time, she prayed for help. She kept her hands on the spot until an inner voice or feeling told her that she had done enough. Soon after, the patient reported that he was completely cured, so much so that he took a job as a gardener.

Probably the world's most famous psychic healer is England's Harry Edwards. Edwards heard the call at a Spiritualist seance, when he was told by the medium that he should use his gifts for psychic healing. Soon afterward he developed trance mediumship and realized that he had been chosen as an instrument to manifest healing from the spirit world. He is convinced that his spirit guides are Drs. Louis Pasteur and Lord Lister, but he attributes the essence of his powers to God.

From time to time Edwards undertakes mass healing services at London's Albert Hall or Royal Festival Hall, which are large enough to hold several thousand people at one time. He welcomes the spotlight of press, radio, and television, and has an impressive record of actual healings performed in the glare of precisely such spotlights. Crippled individuals step up and explain their affliction. He then makes some passes over them or touches their bodies, at the same time praying for divine assistance. Not infrequently, the healing is instantaneous and the crippled person walks off the platform briskly—cured. At other times, several consultations or healing sessions are necessary.

According to M. H. Tester, a British writer on healing, who is a healer himself,

> The oldest and most widely used method of treatment of illness is self-medication. There are hundreds of drugs, medicines, remedies and elixirs on sale without prescription. Many are extensively advertised, and their manufacturers have made fortunes. Yet a man who will regularly fill his body with pills and powders seems incapable of any form of spiritual self-prescription.
>
> Nearly all the patients who come to me seem to have made no effort whatsoever to help themselves except by means of orthodox drug therapy. They are all poor in body, in mind and in spirit. Some may enjoy the outward trappings of wealth, but they are nearly all spiritually impoverished.
>
> I try not to preach to my patients. My job, as I see it, is to heal those who are ready to be healed. If, when they have been made well, they want to know more of the forces that healed them, then I am equipped to show them the road they need to travel.

M. H. Tester is a successful architectural consultant, and was a typical British surburbanite and family man. A few years ago, he suffered a serious spinal injury that left him virtually crippled and in constant pain. In relentless agony, he went from doctor to doctor in search of relief, until an eminent specialist informed him that only a dangerous operation might help his condition. Here providence intervened, and Tester was given the name of a truly remarkable person—a faith healer whom he consequently visited as a desperate last resort. Through this healer, Mr. Tester experienced a healing act of almost biblical intensity, which transformed him in a matter of days from a pain-ridden cripple to a well man.

This powerful experience made him aware that he himself was blessed with healing powers. Making no charge for his services, the former patient became a healer, using his gift to help others enjoy the seemingly miraculous cure he himself had experienced.

Healing is, I discovered, the major component of the teaching of the late "sleeping prophet" Edgar Cayce. Many interesting books have been written about him and his great work is being carried on by his sons at the Association for Research and Enlightenment (ARE) in Virginia Beach, Virginia. Cayce, an untutored photographer, went into trance states during which he was able to diagnose the illnesses of people about whom he knew nothing. The language and contents of these diagnoses were such that only a trained medical doctor could have made them. Nevertheless, Edgar Cayce had no such training, nor was there any fraud or delusion involved. Many of the prescriptions given to the thousands of people who sought Cayce's help turned out to be unknown to the orthodox medical fraternity. Nevertheless, all these remedies worked, and much was learned by those willing to profit from the study of Cayce records.

ARE maintains a special clinic at Phoenix, Arizona, where medical doctors function in accordance with Edgar Cayce material. The clinic is housed in a pleasant suburb of Phoenix, with the mountains as a backdrop. It consists of a complex of one-story buildings and a small garden. By no means comparable to a hospital or a large research establishment, the clinic is nevertheless run along orthodox lines in the sense that patients are seen by appointment, medical records are kept, and the entire operation is undertaken with the full approval and blessing of the Arizona medical authorities.

Dr. William McGarey, who is in charge of the clinic, explains their methods:

In medicine we think in terms of *structure*. We think this man has liver disease, or lung disease, or his heart is abnormal, or he has brain disease, or he has an appendix that is inflamed. The way Cayce talks about it, one of the forces within the body has become unbalanced with the other forces, a system is out of coordination with another system, or the liver is not coordinating in its function with the kidneys because they're both eliminatory organs and the function of elimination has to come about or the individual dies. It is a different approach, from the standpoint of function, and the way we *currently* think about it, the structure is the thing we go by.

11
The Psychic World of Plants

Is it possible to have a meaningful relationship with a plant? Some people (and plants) think so!

An impulsive experiment by lie-detector expert Cleve Backster started the current trend of scientific investigation into plant communication, and many people are getting "curiouser and curiouser" about the flora around us.

Cleve Backster considers himself America's foremost polygraph expert and does in fact work with police departments, both in training personnel and in investigation of difficult cases.

By accident or perhaps by special inspiration, Mr. Backster connected the business end of a polygraph to a plant in his office. More exactly, Backster attached the electrodes of one of his machines to the leaf of a plant called a dracaena, which is a tropical plant somewhat similar to a palm tree, and popularly known as a dragon tree. Backster was interested to see whether watering the plant would show up on the galvanometer, a portion of his equipment. To his surprise, the pen on the graph paper registered a downward trend instead of the expected upward trend. This was in 1966. It started Backster on a whole chain of investigations to ascertain whether there was in fact a sensitive element in plant life that could respond to good or bad treatment, to feelings expressed or unexpressed, to words spoken or thought—in short, whether plants could react to humans.

Eventually, Backster's medical consultant, Dr. Howard Miller, came to the conclusion that some type of cellular consciousness is present in all forms of life, and that it was this basic awareness that caused the plants to react. Backster himself thought that sentience might go down further, all the way to the subatomic level. He devised an apparatus with which experiments could be undertaken without any human beings present. He managed to kill live cells by an automatic device but in the presence of living plants. Sure enough, the plants forced to watch this deliberate cruelty to tropical shrimp registered strongly and with appropriate horror. Backster published his amazing findings in the *International Journal of Parapsychology* in 1968, under the title "Evidence of Primary Perception in Plant Life."

Apparently, as with all ESP phenomena, distance has little or no effect on the results. Backster's experiments seem to indicate that besides some sort of telepathic communication system, plants possess something closely akin to feelings or emotions.

At first, the scientific community tended to dismiss Backster and his apparatus as belonging more properly to the occult sciences, while here and there adventurous parapsychologists got into the act by duplicating "Backster's Effect."

The Backster Effect merely refers to the fact that Mr. Backster has gone down to a level in plants where sentience, or capability of communication, was not previously thought to exist. Perhaps a cellular level, perhaps not. However, if this capability of communication is true, then it prevails with all living things, and the omnipresence of the phenomena and the phenomena themselves would be equivalent to the concept that many people call God. Mr. Backster himself feels that he would be totally embarrassed and out of place to foster that term in any way.

Hans Holzer, in his book *The Psychic World of Plants,* reported the interesting case of Patricia Allen Bott:

"I believe what you think and what you feel can be communicated to the plants around you. I have some plants in my kitchen and sometimes it makes me a little nervous because I can't have a fight with my husband—the plant gets upset. I can't say bad words —the plant doesn't like it. You can see the leaves sort of shut up, curl up, and if I get very mad, the plant vibrates, or reacts, to my feelings, my thoughts. And if I'm mad at someone, the plant becomes afraid. I liked that particular plant because each leaf is different, so I would say to it, 'Come on, everything is all right, let's forget it, come on, grow me a new leaf, I'm sorry.' And sure enough, it would grow a new leaf, and I would understand that I apologized for upsetting it. I think the plant knew that I meant it, and that it had a home that loved it."

Holzer also reported the experience of a Miss Kleveta, who had an African tree in her apartment for six years. When the top of the tree reached almost to the ceiling, the tree stopped growing new leaves, as if it knew it had no place to go. Instead, the trunk, which was one and a quarter inches in diameter, and had been growing straight up until that time, began to bend slowly away from the window and within eight weeks had completely changed direction. By doing this, the tree found more space between the top of the leaves and the ceiling. As soon as the tree had accomplished changing the direction of its trunk, it began to produce new leaves again.

"At first, I did not understand," Miss Kleveta explained. "But the tree must have realized that all new leaves tend to grow toward the light. Then I realized that the tree trunk bent toward the most 'intelligent' direction because had the tree also bent its trunk toward the light, he would have lost balance after a while and toppled over."

I discovered to my amazement how negative the official attitude toward this amazing phenomenon is in some quarters. For instance, the *New York Times* reviewed what is probably the most erudite book on the subject, *The Secret Life of Plants,* by Peter Tompkins and Christopher Beard. This review takes the book to task for presenting acknowledged facts along with new evidence, with such gems as "Kirlian photography is one example of how unexplained fact can shade off into occult fancy," then going on to state that "occultists say the corona effect corresponds to the legendary aura." There is nothing legendary about the aura, nor are occultists its discoverers. Dr. Walter Kilner, a British researcher and physician, discovered it more than sixty years ago. Clearly, the book reviewer of the *New York Times* does not like *The Secret Life of Plants,* or, more accurately, does not like what it represents. And who is this highly qualified reviewer? Why, Elsa Fuerst, whose credentials are those of a child psychologist who sometimes writes for an underground publication called *Changes.*

In the chapter "Plants Can Read Your Mind," Tompkins and Beard come to the conclusion that man communicates with plants, and that plants not only read man's emotions but radiate energy that man can feel in return. In other words, mediumship in a human being could be as effective in attempts at communication with plants as it could be with other human beings or discarnates.

Before long, gardeners and nurseries began to take seriously the matter of possible psychic elements in plants. It took no more than a couple of years for ESP in plants to move from the ludicrous to an exciting topic of conversation.

John Pierrakos, M.D., is one of the scientists currently at work at the Institute of Bioenergetic Analysis in New York City, delving into the energy field of man, animals, plants—and crystals. Pierrakos is a successful practicing psychiatrist and is highly regarded by fellow doctors. I discovered that what goes on inside the Institute of Bioenergetic Analysis is far more significant to the understanding of the nature of man than any purely mechanistic or biochemical study in the past has been. In a scientific paper titled "The Energy Field in Man and Nature," Dr. Pierrakos details his findings, based upon more than twenty years of research. Today he uses his findings, which owe a good deal to the theories of Dr. Wilhelm Reich, in his psychiatric practice as well. By observing the flow of energy, he is able to pinpoint blocks and arrive at more satisfactory diagnoses. But the most significant of all the amazing scientific discoveries made by this doctor is the fact that an aura is not a single emanation of energy but contains several layers of energy, each with a different purpose.

This is how Dr. Pierrakos described the field of the aura of plants:

There are two layers of interaction around the plant surface. The interlayer, immediately surrounding the leaves and branches, is ⅙ to ⅛ of an inch wide with an overall light-blue or gray color. The layer is structured and can be easily seen. The outer layer is much lighter, with an extension of ½ to 1 inch, and has various multicolor radial movements. There are also fireballs that shoot out in space emanating from the outer layer of the field. The colors of the field vary extensively, depending on the species of plant and whether or not the plant is flowering. Flowering plants have a much more extended field, slower pulsation of the field, and greater luminosity around the flowers. For instance, the chrysanthemum has a beautiful sky-blue inner layer, over the flower itself, which is about half an inch wide, and an outer layer of streaming gold rays that extend 3 to 4 inches away from the plant. Cactus plants tend to have a concentrated, deep-blue layer and a streaming, radiant outer layer extending several feet away from the plant. And orchids have a very dark, narrow inner layer with an outer layer made up of beams and rays which resemble a searchlight.

Dr. Pierrakos observed that the pulsations depended on the orientation of the plant or leaf to the geographical cardinal points, and that changing the position of a plant would disturb the pattern of its pulsations.

"The energy field pulsates outwardly, into the surrounding air, for approximately two to four seconds. Following this, there is a reversal of movement and the energy of the surrounding air streams into the plant. I believe that this may play an important part in the process of photosynthesis," reported Dr. Pierrakos.

Some other astounding findings concerning the life energy field of plants: both dead and flowering trees have a slow pulsatory rate, but flowering trees' pulsations are much longer and more sustained. Deciduous trees pulsate twelve to fourteen times a minute, while evergreens do it eighteen to twenty-two times. Perhaps the closest approach to an objective form of gardening in which the interest and desires of plant life are considered along with man's requirements is to be found in *Plants Are Like People* by bestselling author Jerry Baker, which sold more than 150,000 copies in hard cover and millions in paperback. Jerry Baker speaks of plants as if they were people, and *like* people they certainly are. By using familiar terminology and applying it to plants, Baker creates a bond of understanding between master and plant.

The sex life of plants is obviously different from that of humans or animals, especially as it should be kept in mind that plants move at an incredibly slow speed, a speed that has thus far allowed us to ignore much of what goes on among them. But there is movement, and some of it may indeed be sexual. Heliotropism—the ability of plants to move their bodies toward the sunlight—and the ability to attach themselves to walls, trees, or other plants are indications of movement and search for support. Unquestionably, some plants wrap themselves around others not merely to support themselves but perhaps for reasons of affinity.

I heard of an unusual case of a woman in the East who forgot to water her flowers before going away on a long weekend. It was a warm day and the flowers began to wilt. A neighbor, seeing the problem, decided to jump over the garden fence and do what her friend had evidently forgotten in the haste of her departure. When she had finished watering the flower beds, she noticed an almost instant reaction on the part of the dahlias and pompoms: it was as if the blooms were trying to "shine" for her in gratitude. At the same time, her inner ear received the impression of a deep sigh or feeling of peace, for which she could not account rationally.

A similar case concerns a youngster bent on pulling a tulip from its soil. As he extended his hand toward the flower, he noticed, to his utter surprise, that the flower was actually drawing back from him! There was no wind to account for this slight but nonetheless perceptible movement. The young man, a high-school student, had already heard of plant experiments involving ESP, and he put two and two together. Quickly he withdrew his hand and said, "Never mind, I won't take you." Instantly the tulip returned to its former, straight position.

The parallels between human, animal, and plant life are many and compelling. As man and animal subsist on food and drink and air, so plants need water, minerals, and carbon dioxide to live. Men's and animals' bodies convert foodstuffs and water into energy; plants, with the help of sunlight, turn water, minerals taken froom the soil, and other inorganic substances into "food" through the highly intricate process of photosynthesis. Man by himself cannot leave his planet, animals by themselves cannot leave their immediate area of existence, and plants cannot leave the spot where they grow. But all three partake of the same energy field, the same "bioplasma," as Russian scientists have recently labeled it, and it is in the participation in this invisible but very real energy field that man, animal, and plant are partners and mutually connected, if not dependent upon one another.

12
Pyramids and Pyramidology

For centuries a debate has been waged between those who feel that the Great Pyramid of Cheops enshrines a lost science and those who do not. Was this last remaining of the Seven Wonders of the World, often described as the most sublime landmark in history, designed by mysterious architects who had a deeper knowledge of the secrets of this universe than did those who followed them? Though eminent scientists and academicians all agree that the Great Pyramid is at least four thousand years old, none can say for certain just when it was built, by whom, or why.

Recent studies of ancient Egyptian hieroglyphs and the cuneiform mathematical tablets of the Babylonians and Sumerians have established that an advanced science did flourish in the Middle East at least three thousand years before Christ, and that Pythagoras, Eratosthenes, Hipparchus, and other Greeks reputed to have originated mathematics on this planet merely picked up fragments of an ancient science evolved by remote and unknown predecessors.

The Great Pyramid, like most of the great temples of antiquity, was designed on the basis of a hermetic geometry known only to a restricted group of initiates, mere traces of which percolated to the classical and Alexandrian Greeks.

These and other recent discoveries have made it possible to reanalyze the entire history of the Great Pyramid with a whole new set of references: the results are explosive. The common, and indeed authoritative, assumption that the Great Pyramid was just another tomb built to memorialize some vainglorious pharaoh has been proved false.

The pyramid has been shown to be an almanac by means of which the length of the year, including its awkward .2422 fraction of a day, could be measured as accurately as with a modern telescope. It has been shown to be a theodolite, or instrument for the surveyor, of great precision and simplicity, virtually indestructible. It is a compass still so finely oriented that modern compasses are adjusted to it, not vice versa.

It has also been established that the Great Pyramid is a carefully located geodetic marker, or fixed landmark, on which the geography of the ancient world was brilliantly constructed; that it served as a celestial observatory from which maps and tables of the stellar hemisphere could be accurately drawn; and that it incorporates in its sides and angles the means for creating a highly sophisticated map projection of the northern hemisphere. It is, in fact, a scale model of the hemisphere, correctly incorporating the geographical degrees of latitude and longitude. Whoever built the Great Pyramid, it is now quite clear, knew the precise circumference of the planet, and the length of the year to several decimals—data which were not rediscovered until the seventeenth century.

The pyramid's base covers thirteen acres, or seven midtown blocks of the city of New York. From this broad area, leveled to within a fraction of an inch, more than two and a half *million* blocks of limestone and granite—weighting from two to seventy tons apiece—rise in 201 stepped tiers to the height of a modern forty-story building, etched against the cloudless blue of the Egyptian skies.

Near the Pyramid of Cheops stand two more pyramids, one, slightly smaller, attributed to Cheops's successor, Kephren, and another, smaller still, partly sheathed in red granite, attributed to Kephren's successor, Menkure. Together with six diminutive pyramids, supposedly built for Cheops's wives and daughters, they formed what is known as the Giza complex.

No description of the Great Pyramid has survived in the Egyptian texts. Legends have it painted various colors, marked with designs and inscribed with symbols. The first eyewitness descriptions from classical authors survive only in fragmented quotation. Thales, the father of Greek geometry, visited the pyramids sometime in the sixth century B.C. but left no detailed description of his visit. Herodotus, who saw the pyramids about 440 B.C.—by which time they were as ancient to him as his period is to us—said that each of the main structure's four perfectly triangular faces was still covered with a mantle of highly polished limestone.

The Muhammadans' delight in navigation engendered a need for geography, which required astronomy and mathematics. The search for such data was to lead them to the secrets of the Great Pyramid. Abdullah al-Mamun, who came to the throne in A.D. 813, commissioned seventy scholars to produce an "image of the earth" and the first "stellar map in the world of Islam." Al-Mamun was informed that the Great Pyramid was reputed to contain a secret chamber with maps and tables of the celestial and terrestrial spheres. Although they were said to have been made in the remote past, they were supposed to be of great accuracy. In 820 the young caliph collected a vast conglomeration of engineers, architects, builders, and stonemasons to examine the Great Pyramid; for days they searched the steep polished surface of the northern slope for its secret entrance, but could find no trace of it. Not to be thwarted, so the story goes, al-Mamun decided to burrow straight into the solid rock of the structure in the hope of running across some passage in the interior.

For another four centuries the pyramid lay undisturbed on the desert's edge, its outer casing virtually intact, its geometric shadows lengthening and shortening with the revolutions of the years.

Subsequently a series of earthquakes demolished large parts of northern Egypt, and the descendants of al-Mamun's workers wreaked their revenge on the treasureless pyramid by stripping it of its precious limestone casing to rebuild their new capital city, El Kaherah, "The Victorious." In the course of several gene-

it a divine plan for the present root race—the scientific man. It is in itself a measure of scientific precision.

When presented with the problem of construction, the noted psychic and healer Edgar Cayce stated that the stones were put in place by the same methods "that stone can be caused to float in air." The stones fit with one another with less than one-millimeter clearance. Would the use of mere ramps and muscle power be feasible for constant refitting of these heavy blocks? The logistical problems of feeding, clothing, housing, and managing some 400,000 workers seem insurmountable.

The precision of the Great Pyramid defies any classical analysis. In fact, a reasonable guess, based on the evidence, is that the builders possessed a science of which we are totally ignorant. We find in the structure of the pyramid many measurements believed to be unknown until modern times: the position of true north, the exact calculation of the solar year, the weight of the earth, the constant Pi to five places—and many others.

It was not until the turn of the century that mankind even approached an accurate measurement of the distance from the earth to the sun. Yet, to find the number, it is necessary only to multiply by a factor of 10^9 —one billion—the height of the Great Pyramid. It is 149 meters high; the average distance from the earth to the sun is 149 million kilometers.

In June 1974, Patrick Flannagan and his fiancée, Eve Bruce, attended a gathering at a friend's home in Bel Air, California. The guest of honor was a Sufi master—a man from Istanbul named Hassan Shu Shuud. This small man, thin and aging, had flown into Los Angeles for a one-day visit. Immediately upon introduction, Hassan walked directly to Flannagan and placed his index finger in the middle of Flannagan's forehead. "I do not tell the future nor do I flatter," he said. "But I know your future. Not too soon and not too far off you are going to Egypt and when you arrive something will happen that will change your life." In September of that same year, circumstances brought Flannagan and Eve to Cairo. As soon as they arrived, they drove out to the pyramid sites and the following day returned with an Arab guide whom everyone called Champion. Champion is around fifty, has only one eye, and was dressed in the traditional burnoose, augmented with ragged tennis shoes. Flannagan asked him if it would be possible for them to spend the following night in the Great Pyramid. Champion said that not even President Sadat would permit them to sleep in the pyramid. However, just before Flannagan lost all hope, Champion intimated, "All men want money . . ." and Flannagan understood. Champion then instructed them to come to his home at eleven o'clock that evening. They would have a bite to eat and he would prearrange things with the gatekeeper so that they could spend the night inside. He also advised Flannagan to bring plenty of Egyptian money for him.

Champion, with the help of another ten-pound note for the gatekeeper, arranged for their admission. The interior of the pyramid is normally lit throughout the night by fluorescent lamps. But Flannagan—dramatically—requested darkness. With a shrug, the gatekeeper turned off the lights and disappeared into the shadows. A few minutes later, Eve and Flannagan were locked inside for the night. Champion would meet them in the morning.

Flannagan and his fiancée were engulfed in total darkness. They had brought blankets, water, candles, and a powerful flashlight. Flannagan flicked it on and the beam disappeared down the gullet of the Grand Gallery. They paused to catch their breath and then began the long ascent toward the King's Chamber in the heart of the pyramid. "When we arrived at the top step of the Grand Gallery we looked back," Flannagan said later. "It was so huge it just seemed to vanish into the depths of the earth."

The first thing we began to sense was colored lights, blue, green, red, and white. At first I thought they were simply phospheres or luminous impressions one can get due to the excitation of the retina. But what we were really experiencing were actual balls of light that were physically detached from our bodies. I could reach out and almost touch these lights. Then we closed our eyes and resumed our chanting. I felt my body begin to vibrate. I quickly stood up and walked clockwise around the chamber. The lights had disappeared and the flickering candle threw distorted shadows on the ancient stonework. And while chanting, I slowly circled the King's Chamber, from one wall to the next. When I came near the King's coffer, I could feel the ancient initiation processions that possibly occurred there. I was not myself. Suddenly I was not Pat Flannagan! I was changing. My personality was peeling from me like a mask. I felt the whole pyramid engulfing me. . . .

Flannagan then sat on different granite blocks set in the floor of the King's Chamber. Experiencing each block made even stranger feelings come over him. "I felt as though an electric current was racing up and down my spine. It was painful, so painful, in fact, that I went into a sort of catatonic trance." This vibration continued until sometime later when he fell back exhausted.

Although he had read of cases of astral projection, he had never really experienced it until that moment.

I felt myself leave my body, as if I were controlled by some other force. Then I came to a chamber, hidden somewhere deep within the pyramid. This chamber had a vaulted ceiling and inside the room was a pedestal. On this rested a heavy gold book with solid gold pages engraved with odd-looking glyphs. The cover was also engraved with the imprint of human hands. I received the distinct impression that if I were to lay my hands on the pages of that gold book, information from the past would be transmitted directly into my brain. And so when I did just so, I felt a surge of energy assault me. Then I was knocked back into another corner of the chamber. There I noticed that there actually was an entrance to the room, a doorway which was a pivoted stone block. Someday, I remember noting, I would visit this chamber again.

Flannagan was awakened by a deafening and painful roar, which stopped as quickly as it started. Then Eve and Flannagan began to hear a faint chorus of male and female voices. "They were singing some sort of ancient chant—the words were totally unknown to me. It sounded like no language I had ever heard." Then, as they were listening, the chanting faded gently away. He felt pleasant vibrations in his spine and a warm heat engulf him, which lasted throughout the night.

I recently discovered that pyramids played an important role in the professional life of a California dentist, Dr. Paris Garefis, a specialist in oral implants. He explained that he had wanted to test the theory that pyramids "generate some kind of power" to repel bacteria. Reducing bacterial action is the key to speedier patient recuperation, he said.

And so, seventy-two pyramids made from aluminum alloy rods were suspended, with their bases toward the ceiling, over the patient's chair in Dr. Garefis's office in Santa Monica. The environmental-systems company that installed the ceiling fixtures claimed that the pyramid shape "produces an energy field that is beneficial to the human body."

"For the period of a year, the vast majority of my patients have felt less pain and healed quicker than before the pyramids were installed." He stated that it used to take from nine to fourteen days for some patients to be free of pain after oral surgery. "But now," he said, "they're reaching that point in six to ten days!"

Dr. Garefis recalled the case of a busy corporate executive who underwent five hours of grueling dental work: "I thought he was going to wind up in bed. Thanks to the pyramids, however, he made it to a board meeting that day, none the worse for wear."

Pyramidology has become a new "branch" of occult science. Manufacturers of pyramid-shaped devices are doing a flourishing business: people use them to store up energies (while asleep), to heal sore areas of the body, and—sitting under a plastic pyramid for half an hour at a time—to increase their vitality and productivity. Ever since the experiments in the Great Pyramid proved that "something drastic" happens to whatever —or whoever—is exposed *at the center* of the pyramid, we know that "pyramid power" is for real.

Pyramids can be found in many parts of the world, notably in Central America, where they represent a puzzle equal to that of their Egyptian counterparts. Mummies have been found in many (but not all) of the pyramids of Egypt, and, more recently, in those of Central America. This should not surprise anyone, since it has been scientifically demonstrated that a body left for any length of time in a pyramid will *automatically* become mummified.

Undoubtedly, the mummies that have been found were latecomers, interlopers. Possibly later peoples, such as the Egyptians, explored the Central American pyramids after the original builders (the Mayas) had already exhausted their stores and abandoned them. These later peoples could easily have learned the wondrous preservative power of the pyramids and, in their simple-minded quest for immortality, converted these old Mayan storehouses into royal tombs.

At least four pyramids in France have survived up to the present day, those at Plouezoch, Carnac, Falicon, and Couhar. But author R. Charroux believes there must be others, as yet unreported, that "escaped the great destruction ordered by Charlemagne." What secrets might these mute monuments reveal? For one thing, Charroux noted that the pyramids in Brittany "appear to be definitely older" than the Mayan and Egyptian pyramids. He suspects they may be connected to the civilization that flourished on the lost continent of Atlantis, and that a remembrance of this ancient culture still lurks in the human subconscious, vague but persistent.

A Frenchman named Bovis was the first to rediscover the secret of the pyramids. He was in Egypt, visiting the Great Pyramid, when he wondered if there was something intrinsic in the shape of the pyramid itself that preserved or aided in the preservation of bodies. Bovis returned to France and began to experiment carefully and painstakingly. His efforts were rewarded with success. It was really true—the body of a cat, left without any sort of treatment whatsoever, would mummify if left in a particular spot one third of the way up in his scale-model pyramid.

A Czech scientist concluded: "There is a relation between the shape of the space inside the pyramid and the physical, chemical, and biological processes going on inside that space. By using suitable forms and shapes, we should be able to make processes occur faster or delay them."

Bovis's pyramid made no sense at all. The same equipment placed at the same spot on different days revealed completely different patterns each time. What force could cause such totally "unscientific" behavior? What "primitive" people could be expected to understand such a force, let alone make use of it? Are we still expected to believe that these magnificent structures were erected as royal tombs?

Model pyramids are being sold commercially in the United States and in Europe. Small models cost about three dollars and are guaranteed to "sharpen razor blades and dehydrate organic matter" if properly oriented. A large model could sharpen a knife or a machete. And a larger model? A model the size of the Pyramid of Cheops in Egypt, with a volume of 3,360,000 cubic yards . . . or the pyramid at Cholula de Rivaldahia in Mexico, with a volume of 4,300,000 cubic yards—what strength of force could be focused with an energy lens of such vast proportions?

13
Improbable Monuments and Archaeological Puzzles

All over the world there are man-made monuments that do not quite fit into our notions of the times, or that have about them some unusual, baffling quality. Take for instance the Colossus of Memnon. The statue of Memnon—which, incidentally, is not a statue of Memnon but of Pharaoh Amenophis III, or Amenhotep—was erected about 1500 B.C. Its architect was, rather confusingly, also named Amenhotep, son of Hapu. It forms one member of a pair of twin colossi, still standing, about a mile from the western bank of the Nile, among the ruins of Thebes.

The sound that is recorded as having been emitted by the famous "vocal statue of Memnon," was neither constant nor melodious. It came at rare intervals during a two-hundred-period from 20 B.C. to 196 A.D. Infrequently, but always at sunrise, those who stood near it might hear a sound that could be compared to the sound made when a harp string breaks. In thirty-nine references to the time of day at which the sound was heard, eighteen named the time exactly at sunrise. This phenomenon is on record—and was not, it should be noted, a deception. The statue, which had been silent for centuries and has been silent to the present day, appeared to acquire and exercise some strange inherent power of saluting the sun.

Even in their present mutilated, defaced condition, the two colossi are a most impressive sight. Each is some fifty feet high, with about the same distance between them. They sit side by side, looking south-south-east toward the Nile.

The western figure, a single piece of stone, is featureless, and the breast, legs, and feet are badly damaged. The eastern, which is the celebrated "vocal" statue, has obviously suffered far more extensive mutilation. From the pedestal to the waist it is a single block, extensively cracked; from the waist upward it is composed of five tiers of lighter stone, as if foreshadowing that puerile monstrosity, the hundred-foot "statue of Columbus" recently constructed at Palos. As with its fellow, the breast is damaged and the features unrecognizable.

The material of the western statue, and of the lower part of the eastern, is stated to be a "coarse hard gritstone." The upper part of the eastern statue is sandstone.

As already remarked, the eastern statue, which has been to some extent reconstructed, is that which is credited with having once emitted sounds. Before discussing this question, however, it may be well to present a short outline of its history.

The following dates are approximate:

1500 B.C.	Erection of the statues.
524 B.C.	The statues defaced by Cambyses.
27 B.C.	Upper half of the eastern statue thrown down by an earthquake, which also caused additional damage to the western statue.
20 B.C.	Strabo, the historian, visited Thebes, and recorded the fact that, both by report and his own observation, the eastern statue emitted a sound at sunrise.
19 A.D.	The sound heard by Germanicus.
90 A.D.	The sound heard by Juvenal.
130 A.D.	The sound heard by Emperor Hadrian, and by Pausanias.
196 A.D.	Last recorded occasion on which the sound was heard.
(Later)	Eastern statue reconstructed.

The dates on which the sound was heard, as given above, are intended only to provide a few points of reference. During the period 20 B.C.–196 A.D. it seems to have occurred quite frequently, if irregularly—certainly not every morning, but probably at least several times a year.

In South America there are cyclopean ruins everywhere—high on the Andean plateau, on mountaintops, perched on the edges of thousand-foot-high precipices, and even on desolate desert plateaus so high that humans and animals experience difficulty in breathing. These ruins are simply unexplainable without predicating the most modern of stone-cutting tools and means of transportation.

The Spanish conquerors found Incan cities, forts, and palaces built on the foundations and surviving walls of *previous* cultures. These walls are still standing, often with subsequent Incan modifications in evidence. The mysterious race or races that preceded the Incas were apparently not only able to cut and fit enormous monoliths, but they somehow carried the red porphyry blocks incredible distances across mountains, over rivers and mountain torrents, sometimes from quarries more than a thousand miles away, depositing them on cliffs and mountaintops such as Ollantayparubo, Peru, almost as if they had *flown* them there, as the legends suggest. Some of these hard andesite and granite rocks weigh from 150 to 200 tons. Many are covered with intricate carvings, which is also the case with the huge stone buildings and stelae—high commemorative freestanding pillars, like obelisks—in the Mayan lands of Central America.

As far as is known, no precision stone-shaping implements or machines capable of making such multiple fittings of great stones were known to the ancient South Americans, and, for this reason, persistent legends and rumors imply that the ancient builders had developed a "secret ingredient"—a radioactive plant extract that would eat into and dissolve stone, making it fuse itself together or, at least, making the edges malleable. Such an invention, if it existed, would explain the incredible fitting of huge rocks, the intricacy of the handsome carvings, which could have been *molded,* and even the Incan road building, which plunged three-thousand-mile roads in a direct line through mountains, canyons, and all sorts of impossible barriers.

The "impossible" feature of Tiahuanaco, a city of gigantic ruins on the shore of Lake Titicaca, Bolivia, is that it was built at all. It stands on a desolate plateau at an altitude of thirteen thousand feet, a height that causes *soroche,* the dizzying mountain sickness, to people unaccustomed to such heights. It is located too high for corn to grow, for cats to live, for white women to give birth, and certainly too high for a population large enough to have built and carved the enormous stones that comprise the city. In spite of the incredible altitude, a large population must once have lived in the vicinity, as evinced by the terraced hillsides, a deserted port, and extensive ruins nearby.

When the Spaniards arrived at Tiahuanaco, the Quechua and Aymara Indians they found were unable to tell them much about the vast deserted city, except that it had been built by the gods. Upon close examination the Spaniards found that the enormous stone walls of the temples, set upon foundation blocks weighing as much as one hundred tons each, were held in place by silver tenons. The Spanish discoverers enthusiastically removed these tenons in a large-scale construction (or destruction) operation of their own. Unfortunately, many of the walls collapsed in subsequent earthquakes, and a large section of the city, including carved stones and statues, was literally carted away over centuries to make other buildings, including much of the city of La Paz, and also to furnish a road-bed for a railroad. Most of the material remaining was simply too massive to be transported. Nevertheless, enough remains to furnish an archaeological puzzle.

The highest building in the Americas, before the construction of New York's first skyscrapers, was a forgotten Mayan temple in Tikal, Guatemala, now designated simply Tikal IV. Tikal IV, covered by trees, was "lost" for centuries in the jungle, although, shaped more like a steep tower than a pyramid, it soared to a height of 212 feet.

In the Marcahuasi plateau of Peru, large sections of

mountain rock have been carved and modified into the forms of human faces, lions, camels, and what appear to be alligators, hippopotamuses, and also something closely resembling a prehistoric stegasaurus. These carvings are recognizable only at certain times, such as the summer equinox, when the sun, striking them exactly right, brings out their complete features. A seismic cracking of a mountain wall in Paraguay in 1947 revealed an inner "worked" wall about 120 feet high and almost a mile long, but, like other "illogical" South American remains, its hugeness and its inaccessibility make detailed examination difficult and make it easier to classify it as a "natural" wonder.

Stonehenge, with its enormous roofed stone circles with architectural features such as tenons and mortice holes cut into the stone, shows some relationship to the megalithic stonework of Tiahuanaco and other pre-Inca ruins of South America, not only in some of its construction details but in the *reason* for its construction; it is believed that Stonehenge was a gigantic seasonal or astronomical clock, perhaps with other features that we have not yet discovered.

On the large plain of Carnac, in Brittany, there are hundreds of standing stones set in perfectly straight lines. These may have functioned as a calendar, a system of counting, a commemoration of chiefs, or something that we cannot imagine, perhaps connected with astrology.

In Rhodesia stands the unexplained building complex of Zimbabwe, variously thought to be a palace, a temple, a fortress, or the gold mines of King Solomon. It is made of cut stone in a land where cut stone, probably because it was not needed, was never used. But a comparison of the walls of Zimbabwe with those of the mysterious Atlantic Forts of Ireland suggests that they, as well as other megalithic structures in other parts of the world, principally on islands and sea coasts, were built (or planned) by the same people.

During his lifetime, which ended in 1945, Edgar Cayce developed a devoted following through his activities in psychic readings, which solved health problems for people in various parts of the world, many of whom he had never met.

In the course of his psychic readings we find an increasing number of references to Atlantis and to the reappearance of part of it in 1968. A most unusual feature of the Cayce psychic readings about Atlantis was that, when he was not in a trancelike state, he was surprised at his repeated references to Atlantis, and was once quoted as saying: "I wonder where that came from and if there is anything in it?"—a doubt, one might say, widely shared by numerous archaeologists. Nevertheless, he continued to refer to Atlantis in his readings, saying in 1933 that ". . . A portion of the temple [of Atlantis] many yet be discovered under the slime of ages of sea water—near what is known as Bimini, off the coast of Florida." Later, in 1940, he made an exact prediction of the reappearance of part of the western section of Atlantis exactly twenty-eight years in the future: "And Poseidia will be among the first portions of Atlantis to rise again. Expect it in sixty-eight and sixty-nine ['68 and '69]. Not so far away!"

The initial underwater find at the island of Andros, near Pine Key, in 1968, was a rectangular construction outlined by beach grass and sponges, fairly near the surface, divided into several sections by stone partitions. The vestigial walls continue on down beneath the sand, and the flooring, if there is any, has not yet been found.

As more aerial photographs of the area were taken, more underwater "buildings" were found nearby, suggesting a settlement or town or, perhaps, as their numbers grow, a small city. As discovery and investigation continue, with effort to protect these finds from treasure hunters who would like to dynamite them to see what lies beneath, only one thing seems fairly certain—that the builders did *not* construct these buildings underwater, and their present location was once dry land.

Among some of the more sensational finds was that of a "step pyramid" at a depth of twelve fathoms, which was discovered by a charter-boat captain. Other walls have been sighted nearby; fossilized mangrove roots on a three-hundred-foot-long wall gave carbon-dated readings of six thousand to twelve thousand years. Dimitri Rebikoff is reported to have found a wall built around what is now a fresh-water spring, a suggestion that it was a garden pool before the land sank.

Finds such as these have caused considerable re-examination of the waters of the Bahama Banks. Farther out at sea, in much deeper waters, a larger building, occasionally referred to as an underwater pyramid, has been located. It is reported to measure 180 x 140 feet. If it is a pyramid, it is a truncated one, or a temple platform of which only the top is showing.

Charles Berlitz reports another unusual archaeological discovery: "An early-morning fishing party, during a phenomenally low tide passed, north of Newport, on their way to the fishing grounds, a barnacle-encrusted masonry arch coming out of the sea. They neglected to mark it, and search for this arch as well as the tower is still being pursued by the New England Archaeological Research Association."

Among the different sunken lands referred to in antiquity as centers of great civilization there have survived numerous references to lands or mysterious islands in the Atlantic Ocean, past the Pillars of Hercules, at the entrance to (or exit from) the Mediterranean, sometimes called Atlantis or similar-sounding names such as Antilla or referred to as the Fortunate Islands, Islands of the Blessed, or the Hesperides.

The most complete account we have of Atlantis is that of Plato (fifth century B.C.), who described it in two of his famous dialogues, *Timaeus* and *Critias*. This account—studied and commented on for twenty-four hundred years—has given birth to a pro- and anti-Atlantis controversy that has lasted to the present day. In any discussion of prehistory, the evocative word *Atlantis* automatically divides those who immediately classify it as a legend or a hoax from those who on hearing it have an instant vision of ancient grandeur, of an earthly paradise, of lost golden cities lying at the bottom of the ocean, of a continent sinking in a great cataclysm of nature, of survivors fleeing in ships to other parts of the world to preserve a culture, which then became our own. Plato based his account of Atlantis on what he said were actual written records kept by the Egyptian priests of Sais, painted on temple columns. Within the dialogue, Plato gave such exact descriptions of buildings, communication facilities, customs, people, history, topography, and distances that the dialogues seem to fill the function of an ancient "travel guide" to Atlantis.

Among the myriad "proofs" advanced for the existence or nonexistence of Atlantis, a rather nebulous one is perhaps the most convincing. The name Atlantis is itself like a key that almost fits the lock to open the door to past ages. Across the ocean to the New World, we find that the ancient Aztecs told the Spanish conquistadores that their ancestors, the people of Az, came from Aztlan, a sunken land in the east, and that the "fair god" Quetzalcoatl, a white-bearded teacher, had also come from a land in the sea called Tollan-Tlallapan. Another linguistic coincidence appears when we consider that the Aztec word for "water"—atl— also means "water" in Berber, the language of a non-Arabic people who inhabit the Atlas Mountains of North Africa.

The Canary Islands, where an ancient survival race was found (and exterminated), and the Azores, where statues, plaques, and underwater ruins have been reported, are considered by some researchers to be the mountain peaks of the sunken Atlantean continent. Although Atlantis has been "located" in many parts of the world, considerably more than a third of the sites are in the sunken plateau around the Azores, possibly including the Madeira and Canary Islands (whose original inhabitants thought they were survivors of Atlantis).

Fairly recent investigations by American scientists and oceanographers seem to corroborate the theory of submerged Atlantic lands. Professor Ewing of Columbia University found evidence that lava had spread only recently on the bottom of the ocean, and stated: "Either the land must have sunk two to three miles or the sea once must have been two to three miles lower than now. Either conclusion is startling." Professor Bruce Heezen, on a Duke University project concerning the Puerto Rico Trench, identified coral reefs at extreme depths, and observed: "Coral reefs don't grow in more than fifty feet of water. This means that the area we studied once had to be near sea level."

Ruins found on Pacific islands, of which the present inhabitants conserve only vague legends, have given rise to popular speculation that such islands must be the remains of another lost continent. Such a continental land mass must have existed, it is reasoned, to explain the hundreds of cyclopean statues and structures on Easter Island, whose present area would support only a small population; the huge stone city on Ponape in the Carolines; and stone ruins and roads running into the sea on other Pacific islands. Memories and legends of this empire have persisted down to modern times, as demonstrated by the tribute payments involving Yap, Truk, and other islands, whereby islanders would deliver tribute to far-off points without knowing exactly why, except that it would be tabu *not* to do so.

The deserted city of uncertain date on Ponape, whose size and construction give evidence of a former powerful and well-organized culture that vanished almost without echoes, Nan Madol, also called Metalanim (or Metaranimu during the long Japanese rule of the Carolines), covers more than eleven square miles, crisscrossed by canals and constructed of huge, perfectly cut basalt blocks, transported from quarries thirty miles away. Some of its walls are forty feet high and eighteen feet thick. A most unusual feature of its construction is that the canals apparently were built up instead of down, and the islands themselves are largely artificial, being actually stone platforms laid in the ocean. Stone was laid on the top of the coral reefs to form a series of connected islands and canals. Huge breakwaters to protect the city were laid in the ocean itself, and a sea gate permitted the great canoes access to the sea.

An outstanding example of cultural regression among the peoples of the Pacific islands is the loss of the Easter Island system of writing before it could be translated. When Easter Island was first visited, some of the islanders in a population of perhaps six thousand could still read the mysterious *rongo-rongo* writings, written or carved on flat boards and also carved on rocks. It seems to be a syllabic alphabet; some of the characters represent human figures, and others are line figures of simple design. After the depredations of slavery and disease, when the population was reduced to about one hundred, everyone who once could read had died off and with them the secret of the "alphabet" and the contents of the records. Other similar writing, equally undecipherable, has been found in the Caroline Islands.

The mystery of how the great lava-stone statues at Easter Island were put into place has been partially solved by Thor Heyerdahl, during his investigations there. On Easter Island, isolated in the Pacific 2,350 miles off the coast of Chile, are almost six hundred enormous stone statues, called *moai,* showing the torsos and heads of enigmatic figures, some of which measure about four stories in height and weigh up to fifty tons each. They were originally set on stone platforms, and on their flat heads were balanced huge red-colored stone topknots; they were cut and transported from a distant quarry. Most of these statues have been tipped over, losing their topknots, and others have had their phalluses broken off. Still others lie in the original quarry, where they were evidently still being produced when some disaster overtook their sculptors.

The beginning of writing of any sort—whether markings carved or notched in reindeer or other bones, painted on or carved in stone, incised in clay, or painted on walls of caves—is constantly being revised backward in time. Some inscriptions found in Western Europe are of such great age that, although the objects are genuine, it is considered that it cannot have been writing. A piece of reindeer bone from a cave at Rochebertier, France, contains some symbols that seem to resemble the unknown inscription of the ring from Tartessus, while antlers from caves at Le Mas d'Azil and La Madeleine are also inscribed with signs resembling Phoenician letters.

Even more remarkable are the larger "alphabet"

finds of Glozel unearthed in 1924 near Vichy, France, which have been the subject of debate ever since. Among bricks, axes, pottery, and tablets of the Magdalenian era, one incised tablet in particular shows a collection of signs or letters, several of which are equivalent to Phoenician or Greek, while others are unidentifiable. Clearly defined writing of this era and in such a location is archaeologically unacceptable, and although the Glozel tablets have been vouched for by many prehistorians, the mystery still stands. A mystery that, if verified, would indicate that unknown people in northern Europe were able to write thousands of years before the Egyptians first developed their hieroglyphic script—a most unsettling concept to traditional archaeology.

The concept of lost ages of civilization, of advanced cultures so far back in the past that they do not fit in any previously established pattern of civilization, is naturally looked upon with skepticism, suspicion, and sometimes alarm by the scientific and archaeological establishments. An understandable desire on the part of experts to keep things within their established boundaries, however, does not mean that new information will not alter previous concepts.

England is full of strange, puzzling artifacts. Take the grooved monolith of Duddo, Northumberland, for instance. This is not, in fact, a free-standing stone but one of a number forming the Duddo Stone Circle. This stone is singled out because its grooving is so strikingly emphatic. Once again, there is speculation as to whether this is natural grooving, the result of thirty or forty centuries of weathering on this bleak Northumbrian hilltop, or the result of sword-sharpening in the Middle Ages when border warfare was at its height. It can hardly be proved, one way or the other, but the first seems the most likely explanation. Whichever is the answer, however, the carving on this shapely monolith merits the closest scrutiny; it varies with the time of day; you might take a score of photographs in close-up and obtain a different "portrait" with every exposure.

An unusual "inscribed" stone at Roughtinglinn,

Northumberland, also merits mention. This magnificent specimen is on a hillside in a remote corner of this northernmost county, some six miles southeast of the Duddo Stone Circle; it is well worth the search. But one will be puzzled by the series of targetlike concentric circles, a foot and more in diameter, skillfully inscribed in the face of this vast tilted slab of rock. The pattern is sometimes known as "cup-and-ring," and each may be linked by a straight or wavy line to its neighbor. It is almost certainly Bronze Age in origin, though this cannot be proved. Similar inscribed slabs in Spain have been held to be symbolic of the Earth Mother, or Earth Goddess.

Atop a wooded hill in North Salem, N.H., stands a complex of ruins that has defied proper identification for many years. But recently Professor Barry Fell of Harvard confirmed, by Professor Hans Holzer's earlier independent research, that Mystery Hill is a giant megalithic astronomical complex built four thousand years ago by Celt-Iberian and Phoenician travelers.

The land upon which this megalithic complex stands was purchased in 1957 by Robert E. Stone of Derry, N.H., for the purposes of preservation and research. During the last twenty years, research has been conducted on many fronts, and this site is now regarded as possibly the oldest manmade stone complex in the United States and potentially the most important archaeological site in the country.

It is obvious that the structures are not at all characteristic of Indian or Colonial construction habits; hence, the idea that they may have been built by regional native Americans has been dismissed. Through means of comparative archaeology, however, we find virtually identical Bronze Age structures in Portugal, Spain, and Ireland, giving substantial credence to the theory that Mystery Hill is an authentic megalithic structure from antiquity.

The first solid piece of evidence of the site's antiquity emerged in 1969, when a charcoal sample was located and analyzed by the radiocarbon dating method. The result was an age determination of three thousand years. In 1970, an additional radiocarbon age determination resulted in proof that Mystery Hill was occupied at least four thousand years ago.

Some of the more sophisticated stone structures in the world, like Stonehenge in England, were in fact utilized as "Neolithic computers." They were built by an ancient people well-versed in mathematical astronomy. After the institution of precise research methods, it was determined that Mystery Hill was, and is, at the very least, a system for determining the exact locations of solar, lunar, and polestar events, to include the annual equinoxes and solstices. The standing stones along the circumference of the site can still be utilized today to note these celestial events.

Research in epigraphy and anthropology has resulted in the final pieces of the puzzle falling into place. The question of the site's exact age is now in the final stages of being answered; for in 1975 ancient stone inscriptions in the Celt-Iberian, Punic, and Ogham script were deciphered and translated. These inscriptions were in scripts used only by the ancient Phoenicians and Celts in the Iberian Peninsula in pre-Christian times, and have been dated to at least 800 B.C.

Located in the center of this megalithic complex is the famous "sacrificial table," a four-and-a-half-ton grooved slab supported by stone legs. A speaking tube, through which a voice can be channeled, exists directly under this giant granite slab from the large "oracle chamber" behind it.

Among the many structures is the "tomb of lost souls," believed to be an ancient burial tomb.

On the first day of winter each year, December 21, the sun sets on the "winter solstice monolith" when viewed from a platform near the center of the complex. This standing stone, plus many other astronomically oriented monoliths, has made it possible to label the site "America's Stonehenge."

During 1974–75, it was determined that this stone was lined up with the polestar Thuban around 2000 B.C. and is on the main central axis from which the other alignments were determined.

Similar in shape to the "winter solstice monolith," the sun sets directly on this standing stone, over five hundred feet away, seen from the central viewing position each June 21. Similar stones are positioned correctly for the sunrises.

I discovered that there are a number of inscribed stones found at Mystery Hill. Among them are two stones translated by Professor Barry Fell in 1975:

> This inscription is in Iberian Punic and reads, "embellished by" . . . (first line) and "hewed this stone-work" or "cut this stone" (second line). The name of the individual is broken off the stone. (Found around 1960.)

> Pictured about is a badly eroded votive tablet with a monogram of "Bel" in Iberian Punic and Ogham. (Found in 1975.)

14
The Bermuda Triangle

The Bermuda Triangle is one of the most disturbing and almost unbelievable of the world's mysteries. This area is in the western Atlantic, off the southeast coast of the United States, forming what has been termed a triangle, extending from Bermuda in the north to southern Florida, then west to a point through the Bahamas, past Puerto Rico, to about forty degrees west latitude, and then back again to Bermuda. Here, more than one hundred planes and ships have literally vanished into thin air, most of them since 1945. In the past twenty-six years, more than one thousand lives have been lost, and not a single body or even a piece of wreckage from the vanishing planes or ships has been found. Even with today's heavy sea and air travel, carefully kept records, and thorough searches, the disappearances in this area continue to occur frequently.

On December 5, 1945, a group of five planes (Navy TBM Avengers) disappeared while on a mission from Fort Lauderdale Naval Air Station. When a Martin Mariner was sent on the rescue mission, it also disappeared. One of the most intensive ground-sea rescue operations ever conducted failed to locate a life raft, or oil slick, or wreckage.

Many of the planes have disappeared while in radio contact with their base or destination until the very moment they simply vanished. Other aircraft, including passenger planes, have vanished while receiving landing instructions, almost as if, as mentioned in the Naval

Board of Inquiry procedures, "they had flown through a hole in the sky." Others have radioed strange messages, implying that their instruments were not functioning, that their compasses were spinning, and that the sky had turned yellow and hazy (on a clear day), and that the ocean (which was calm nearby) "didn't look right," without further clarification of what was wrong.

Large and small boats have disappeared without leaving wreckage, as if they and their crews had been snatched into another dimension. Large ships, such as the *Marine Sulphur Queen,* a 425-foot freighter, and the *U.S.S. Cyclops,* nineteen thousand tons with 309 people aboard, have simply vanished, while other ships and boats have been found drifting within the Triangle, sometimes with an animal survivor such as a dog or canary, who could give no indication of what had happened—although in one case a talking parrot vanished along with the crew.

It is true, of course, that many planes fly over the Triangle every day, that large and small ships sail its waters, and that countless travelers visit the area every year *without* incident. Granted, ships and planes are lost in all the world's seas and oceans for a variety of reasons (and we must remember to differentiate between "lost at sea," which suggests the finding of wreckage or some identifiable flotsam, and "disappeared," which implies none at all), but in no other area have the unexplained disappearances been so numerous.

It has long been known in maritime circles that many ships have disappeared in this area, and some of these may have contributed to the legend of the "Sea of Lost Ships" or the "Ships' Graveyard," located in the Sargasso Sea, part of which lies within the Triangle. Records concerning lost ships seem to indicate disappearances with increasing frequency since the 1860s.

Of all the cases I've investigated concerning the Bermuda Triangle, the most intriguing is the disappearance of six Navy planes and their crews on December 5, 1945. The first five planes that disappeared, apparently simultaneously, were on a routine training mission starting at the Naval Air Station at Fort Lauderdale, Florida, then 160 miles to the east, 40 miles to the north, and then back to their base following a southwesterly course.

Flight 19 was the group of doomed planes that left Fort Lauderdale on the afternoon of December 5, 1945. Carlton "Sam" Hamilton was on duty as an airport-traffic control tower operator at Miami International Tower during the time that Navy Squadron Flight 19 went out and did not come back. Hamilton, now chief airport-traffic controller, Opalaka ATC, Opalaka, Florida, has been involved in commercial aviation for roughly twenty-five years. As he recalls that night, the squadron departed from Fort Lauderdale on an instrument flight plan. Miami Tower handled this flight on the initial phase just east of Miami and lost contact with it.

The weather was fair for the south Florida area and there were only a few tenuous clouds that day. There were other planes flying in cross-patterns over the area. Most of these craft flew at a higher altitude than the fighter aircraft. As Mr. Hamilton recalled, "The flight went out at four thousand feet, then was supposed to climb to about six thousand feet. In 1945 most commercial aircraft flew at an altitude of eight to twelve thousand feet."

A routine instrument flight-plan-conversation preceded the loss of communication. Instrument flight plans give the aircraft the authority to fly at a certain altitude and tell the flight leader what course to follow. Mr. Hamilton had no indication whatsoever that anything was wrong. The planes were manned by five officer pilots and nine enlisted crew members, the latter detailed two to each plane but on this day short one man, who had requested removal from flying status *because of a premonition,* and who had not been replaced. The planes were Navy Grumman TBM-3 Avenger torpedo bombers, and each carried enough fuel to enable it to cruise more than a thousand miles. The temperature was sixty-five degrees, the sun was shining, and there were scattered clouds and a moderate northeast wind. Pilots who had flown earlier that day reported ideal flying weather.

At about 3:15 P.M., after a practice bombing run had been accomplished and the planes had continued east, the radioman at the Fort Lauderdale Air Station Tower, who had been expecting contact from the planes regarding estimated time of arrival and landing instructions, received an unusual message from the flight leader. The record shows the following:

Flight Leader (Lieutenant Charles Taylor): Calling Tower. This is an emergency. We seem to be off course. We cannot see land. . . . Repeat . . . We cannot see land.

Tower: What is your position?

Flight Leader: We are not sure of our position. We cannot be sure just where we are. . . . We seem to be lost. . . .

Tower: Assume bearing due west.

Flight Leader: We don't know which way is west. Everything is wrong. . . . Strange . . . We can't be sure of any direction—even the ocean doesn't look as it should. . . .

It became increasingly difficult to hear messages from Flight 19 because of static. Apparently, Flight 19 could no longer hear messages from the tower, but the tower could hear conversations among the planes. Some of these messages referred to possible fuel shortages—fuel for only seventy-five miles—references to seventy-five-mile-per-hour, and the unnerving observation that every gyro and magnetic compass in all the planes was off—"going crazy," as it was reported at the time—each showing a different reading. During all this time the powerful transmitter at Fort Lauderdale was unable to make any contact with the five planes, although the interplane communications were fairly audible.

By this time, personnel at the base were in an understandable uproar as news spread that Flight 19 had encountered an emergency. There were all kinds of suppositions concerning enemy attack (although World War II had been over for several months) or even attacks by new enemies, and rescue craft were dispatched, notably a twin-engined Martin Mariner boat-patrol plane with a crew of thirteen, from the Banana River Naval Air Station. Some reports claim that the last words heard from Flight 19 were "It looks like we are . . ." Although other listeners seem to remember more, such as: "Entering white water . . . We are completely lost. . . ." No further message was ever received from Flight 19.

Another plane involved in the incident was a PBY carrying thirteen men that went out to search for the fighter aircraft. This plane was in contact with the Miami Air Traffic Control Center for a while, but, after finishing a transmission, the tower tried to contact the aircraft again and there was no return answer.

I learned from Sam Hamilton that there were other planes, too. A C-46 aircraft was coming in to Miami around three in the morning. "The flight had been turned over to me by Miami Air Route Traffic Control Tower, which is routine when the aircraft is roughly forty-five to sixty miles out. I had been chatting with the pilot, had issued him a clearance on to Miami, and also the descent from the altitude of six thousand feet, when all of a sudden I called the aircraft again and again but there was no response." Then Air-Sea Rescue and several other military units called the aircraft. But no further transmission was ever received from it, nor was any oil slick or other trace of the aircraft ever found.

Mr. Hamilton has believed all along that the pilot of the C-46 should have been able to see some lights from the city of Miami. "Of course, in those days," says Mr. Hamilton, "there were not nearly as many lights, nor was there the kind of continuation of lights that we see today extending from Homestead to Vero Beach. But apparently there were not enough lights for the pilot to see the shoreline, for if he had been able to, certainly he would have at that altitude tried to make the shoreline."

Search and Rescue was called out within fifteen minutes after contact with the aircraft was lost. They searched the general area for an hour, and a larger search went on for days afterward, but to no avail. Nothing was ever found.

Mr. Hamilton believes that there is some strange phenomenon that happens up to 150 miles off the Florida coast and between the altitude of ten thousand feet and sea level. This phenomenon, he said, is "not there all the time, but under certain conditions—it could be atmospheric conditions, it could be conditions that affect the navigation or the ability for a piece of equipment to function properly—and possibly there only for a short period of time, and then gone again."

On July 3, 1947, a U.S. Army C-54, carrying a crew of six on a routine flight from Bermuda to Morrison Army Air Field, Palm Beach, disappeared somewhere between Bermuda and Palm Beach, its last position being about 100 miles off Bermuda. An immediate, intensive air-sea search by Army, Navy, and Coast Guard units covered over 100,000 square miles of sea, although (except for some seat cushions and an oxygen bottle, which were *not* identified as equipment from the lost plane) no wreckage or oil slick was sighted.

As further disappearances occurred, a somewhat alarming feature was noted: the majority of incidents in the Triangle area seemed to take place during the peak tourist and hotel season, from November to February. Even more startling was the realization that many of the losses occurred within a few weeks of Christmas. A British South American Tudor IV four-motor passenger plane, a converted Lancaster bomber, called the *Star Tiger*, flying from the Azores to Bermuda, disappeared on January 29, 1948. It carried a crew of six, and twenty-five passengers, including Sir Arthur Cunningham, a British World War II air marshal and former commander of the Second Tactical Air Force of the R.A.F. The *Star Tiger* was scheduled to land at Kindley Field, Bermuda, and at 10:30 P.M., shortly before ETA (estimated time of arrival), the pilot radioed the control tower a message including the words "Weather and performance excellent" and "expect to arrive on schedule." The plane's position was reported as 380 miles northeast of Bermuda. There was no further message, and the *Star Tiger* never arrived.

As the search continued, without success, numerous ham-radio operators along the Atlantic coast and even farther inland picked up a garbled message with the words spelled out by numbered dots—as if someone was working the sender but did not know Morse code. The dots spelled out "Tiger." Even more weird was a report from a Coast Guard station in New Foundland. As the taps stopped, someone had apparently sent a verbal message—simply pronouncing the following letters: g-a-h-n-p. These were the call letters of the lost *Star Tiger*.

Smaller planes also have continually disappeared. In December 1949 alone, at least nine vanished off the coast of Florida. This number might be sufficient to cause one to reflect that there was something dangerous about the area even if the pattern of disappearances had not been fairly obvious.

During the 1950s, planes continued to disappear. In March 1950, a U.S. Globemaster disappeared on the northern end of the Triangle while on its way to Ireland. On February 2, 1952, a British York transport, carrying thirty-three passengers and crew, vanished on the northern edge of the Triangle while on its way to Jamaica. Some weak signals were received but were almost immediately aborted.

On October 30, 1954, a U.S. Navy Constellation disappeared with forty-two passengers and crew while flying in fair weather from Patuxent River Naval Air Station, Maryland, to the Azores. More than two hundred planes and many surface vessels joined in searching several hundred square miles of ocean, but nothing was found. As in the case of some of the other planes, a scarcely identifiable SOS was received shortly after the plane's disappearance.

A U.S. Air Force KB-50 tanker leaving from Langley Air Force Base, Virginia, on its way to the Azores, on January 8, 1962, disappeared, as had the Super Constellation lost in 1954. Again, as with the Super Constellation, there was a weak radio message indicating an unspecified difficulty, and then silence—and, following the pattern, no wreckage or any indication as to what had happened. It must be remembered that in each disappearance the crews had ample lifesaving equipment in case of ditching, so whatever happened to the planes happened unexpectedly and extremely quickly.

Despite all modern improvements, odd incidents and

losses continue to occur in the Triangle area. Within
the past few years, several planes mysteriously disinte-
grated over land within a short distance of Miami International Airport, including Eastern Airlines Flight
401 (a Lockheed L-1011), with a loss of over one hundred passengers and crew on December 29, 1972.

Long before the aircraft incidents of the 1940s, the
area encompassed in the Bermuda Triangle—including
Cape Hatteras, the coasts of the Carolinas, and the
Florida Strait—had often been referred to as the "Ships'
Graveyard," the sinkings usually being caused by heavy
seas and sudden storms. The Sargasso Sea is also referred to as the "Ships' Graveyard," or the "Sea of
Lost Ships," for an opposite reason: ships have been
lost there not in storms but in calms. Within this general area, certain mysterious disappearances of large
ships, without sending SOS signals and without subsequent findings of flotsam or bodies, have already been
noted through the years, but it was not until the mass
plane disappearances of 1945 and thereafter and the
sudden disappearances of large and small boats that
researchers began to consider the pattern recurrent.

Crews and passengers have frequently vanished from
smaller boats, later found abandoned and adrift, such
as the yacht *Connemara IV*, found 400 miles southwest
of Bermuda in September 1955, empty of passengers
and crew; the sixty-foot *Maple Bank*, found drifting
north of Bermuda on June 30, 1969, with no trace of
survivors; the *Vagabond*, a twelve-meter owner-
operated yacht found adrift but otherwise ship-shape
west of the Azores on July 6, 1969, with no sign of its
owner, Captain Wallace P. Williams, or its crew. Some
boats have disappeared on fairly short trips, such as the
yacht of Al Snyder, a well-known jockey, who took
several of his friends on his cabin cruiser out of Miami
on March 5, 1948, to go fishing at Sandy Key; although
the yacht was later found, the occupants had disappeared.

The loss of a 425-foot freighter, the *Marine Sulphur
Queen*, with a crew of thirty-nine, on or about February
2, 1963, is particularly striking because of the size of

the vessel. It was bound for Norfolk, Virginia, from Beaumont, Texas, with a cargo of fifteen thousand long tons of molten sulphur carried in steel tanks. The weather was good. The ship was last heard from at a point near the Dry Tortugas, in the Gulf of Mexico, an area in or near the Triangle according to its somewhat elastic boundaries.

A Marine board of investigation noted that the *Marine Sulphur Queen* had "disappeared at sea without the transmission of a radio distress message," but offered neither solution nor theory concerning this disaster.

Joe Talley, captain of a fishing boat, the *Wild Goose*, experienced a different, though not, in his case at least, fatal, disappearance within the Triangle. His boat was in tow behind another boat, in the Tongue of the Ocean, an area within the Bahama group but not part of the Bahama Banks. Its relatively small area is thousands of feet deep; a precipitous drop-off directly east of Andros Island, it has been the site of many disappearances.

Captain Talley's 65-foot shark-fishing vessel was to be towed south in the Tongue of the Ocean by the 104-foot *Caicos Trader*. It was nighttime and Captain Talley was asleep in his bunk below decks. Suddenly he was awakened by a flood of water pouring over him. He automatically grabbed a life jacket and fought his way to an open porthole. As he forced his way out, he found that he was under water but he encountered a line and followed it to the surface, a distance estimated as between fifty and eighty feet. He had apparently been submerged forty to fifty feet when he escaped from his quarters.

When he got to the end of the line, and the surface, he found that the *Caicos Trader* had continued on its way without him. What had happened was that the sudden force that was drawing the *Wild Goose* under water toward the bottom, with Captain Talley on board, was threatening to capsize the *Caicos Trader* because of the connecting towline. The crew of the towboat cut the towline, left the immediate area, and then turned about to see if by some miracle Talley had managed to escape from the cabin of his craft as it was drawn down beneath the sea. The crew of the towboat had seen the *Wild Goose* go straight down "as if in a whirlpool."

The experience of Captain Don Henry, in 1966, gives a graphic account of a "tug of war" between a towboat and an unidentified force attempting, consciously or unconsciously, to capture the barge. Charles Berlitz reported the captain's testimony:

". . . We were coming in on the return trip between Puerto Rico and Fort Lauderdale. We had been out for three days towing an empty barge which had carried petroleum nitrate. I was aboard the *Good News*, a hundred-and-sixty-foot-long tug of two thousand horsepower. The barge we were towing weighed twenty-five hundred tons and was on a line a thousand feet behind. We were on the Tongue of the Ocean, after coming through the Exumas. The depth was about six hundred fathoms.

"It was afternoon, the weather was good, and the sky was clear. I had gone to the cabin in back of the bridge for a few minutes when I heard a lot of hollering going on. I came out of the cabin onto the bridge and yelled, 'What the hell is going on?' The first thing I looked at was the compass, which was spinning clockwise. There was no reason that this should ever happen—the only place besides here I ever heard it to happen was in the St. Lawrence River at Kingston, where a big deposit of iron or maybe a meteorite on the bottom makes the compasses go crazy. I did not know what had happened, but something big was sure as hell going on. The water seemed to be coming from all directions. The horizon disappeared—we couldn't see where the horizon was— the water, sky, and horizon all blended together. We couldn't see where we were.

"Whatever was happening robbed, stole, or borrowed everything from our generators. All electric appliances and outlets ceased to produce power. The generators were still running, but we weren't getting any power. The engineer tried to start an auxiliary generator but couldn't get a spark.

"I rammed the throttles full ahead. I couldn't see where we were going, but I wanted to get the hell out in a hurry. It seemed that something wanted to pull us back, but it couldn't quite make it.

"Coming out of it was like coming out of a fog bank. When we came out the towline was sticking out straight—like the Indian rope trick—with nothing visible at the end of it where it was covered by a fog concentrated around it."

I have gathered other firsthand accounts of actual witnesses, people who know what it feels like to pass through the area and come out again *alive*.

Frank Flynn, now a licensed real estate salesman in Fort Lauderdale, spent over twenty years in the Coast Guard and achieved the rank of commander.

In 1956 he was doing a tour of duty on the *Yamacroft* and was sailing in the Bermuda Triangle area. One calm, clear night, just before midnight, he came on watch. At about one-thirty in the morning he glanced at the radarscope and a solid green line caught his eye, so he called over his assistant, the quartermaster of the watch, and asked him what he thought. The assistant was surprised and said that it looked like land. Flynn agreed and ran a recheck of their course. Everything seemed in order.

When Flynn first spotted the green line, he said, he marked it on the scope with a grease pencil and fifteen minutes later checked it again. "The line was dead in the water because it had moved proportionately to our speed toward it."

At that point he called the commanding officer to the bridge. Captain Strouch, who had twenty-five years in the service, told them they were 100 to 160 miles offshore. He then personally rechecked position and plotted the speed of advance.

". . . So we continued on," said Frank Flynn. "The captain stayed on the bridge. We approached the unknown radar target rather carefully. When we got down to about three hundred yards from it we started making a turn so as to parallel it so we could pull away fairly rapidly in case it was solid. We shone a searchlight into the unknown substance and it appeared to be a clay wall. It was surprising for me to see this gray mass just sitting there in the perfectly clear and calm night. We shone the light vertically and could find no end. Then we ran parallel to it for fifteen to twenty minutes. We than moved closer and pointed the starboard point of the bridge into it and nothing happened so we came back out and turned into it at cruising speed."

As they continued on, they pointed the carbon light into the object but could see only a dull glow. They also felt throat irritation and had difficulty breathing. Soon the engine room had a problem with steam pressure. Just as Captain Strouch had ordered a left full rudder to back out, the ship's bow broke through and was finally on the other side of the object. They then ran parallel to it on the other side. Frank Flynn estimated the mass to be about a thousand feet thick.

The incident ended as the Coast Guard cutter emerged from the gray bank. When I talked to Frank Flynn, his final comment was he had never seen anything like "it" before or since. He did not consider the phenomena frightening. He found his own feelings strange and indicated that he has always wondered if the facile explanation that the wall was a fog bank sufficed to describe what his ship had penetrated. For me his story was another indication that travellers in the Bermuda Triangle might encounter phenomena that are strange and unexplainable.

After I left Frank Flynn, I met Ray Smithers, former production manager of WFTL, who became interested in the Bermuda Triangle through a book of Edgar Cayce's and his predictions of Atlantis that involve the Triangle. "WFTL started a series on the Bermuda Triangle because the station is located in the alleged Triangle and local residents have a tremendous interest in it," said Mr. Smithers. "They hear local news stories about people being lost, day after day. So when the national publicity level got very active on the Triangle, WFTL decided to run an investigatory series. We had experts on the show, giving opinions and trying to explain in depth what all the Triangle theories are. Since these theories were very difficult and involved scientific theories, we did it over a period of six shows, six weeks, three hours every Sunday night.

"One thing we learned from the show, which surprised us, is that every person you come across has another opinion of the Triangle. We had people call in and say, 'It's awfully good to hear that somebody else had a strange experience because I did and I never told anybody in the world about it, I'm afraid of being called a kook.'"

One of those strange experiences involved a commercial airline pilot who talked about a time-warp, the fact that they should have landed at a given time and according to their watches and all the chronometers on the instruments in their cockpit they were landing perfectly on time. In fact, when they got out of the plane —and there were allegedly some forty passengers on the flight from one of the islands to Fort Lauderdale— they had lost an hour and fifteen minutes against the tower clock and couldn't account for it. The pilot would not give his name and would not say what airline he was with when he called the radio station.

I was surprised to learn that ninety-nine percent of the people calling in stories would not give their names. Those who did, however, would not give a commercial name of an airline or boat.

During the second broadcast in the series there was a strange experience. "Allen Moore was the co-host, Page Bryant, a psychic who has done psychical research on the Triangle, was there, and on a telephone from his home in Miami was Manson Valentine, an oceanographer and paleontologist, who has a lot of theories on the Triangle. We were technically to tie in outside phone calls on the air with Mr. Valentine's call, plus we could all hear it in the studio.

"About forty-five minutes into the broadcast normally all the phone lines are blinking, they're all solid, we had hundreds and hundreds of calls. During any given broadcast there was never an open line that was not ringing. About forty-five minutes into the broadcast Allen Moore went to answer a call and hit the first line. It was blinking as though a call was coming in and there indeed was no one there, there was no sound as though someone was on the phone, just dead. He proceeded to go down five additional lines and they were all in the same condition. Finally on the sixth line our caller started making a statement. We found it strange immediately because most people say, 'Hello, Allen, hello. It's nice to be on the air.' Most people preface their statement this way but this person just started making his statements. At the time it happened, Page Bryant looked at me, I looked at her, we had kind of a physical-mental reaction. It just seemed strange at the moment, is the only way I can put it. The caller went on to expound a theory about the Triangle that we were all unfamiliar with. When Page started to talk back to him, to develop a conversation, the line went dead and the dial tone came up. Usually when a person calls in, the line stays dead for a long, long time before the dial tone comes back. We heard click and about four seconds went by and then we heard a dial tone immediately. The people around the station thought it was strange in the sense that we didn't think it was a normal phone quality. We'd been listening three hours through several shows to people calling in from all different kinds of phones and areas and the voice quality seemed quite different as well.

"The day after the broadcast the morning DJ offhandedly made a general reference to the Bermuda Triangle show. Immediately eight unconnected lines lit up the switchboard at the same moment. The people calling explained that they had physical or mental reactions from the strange voice of the mystery caller. In the next twenty minutes about twenty-five phone calls were received from different kinds of people, different ages, both men and women. Later we started playing some of these tapes on the air. This prompted many more people to call, and in the next two days WFTL received several hundred phone calls."

The claims people made about the voice were varied. "The one we heard most often was the fact that people were depressed the minute they heard the voice," said Mr. Smithers. "A lot of people did relate something to what the voice said and actually got teary-eyed and several women and one man cried when they heard the voice. They couldn't explain it any more than we could. Page Bryant and I that night had the same kind of experience. It was slightly depressing but other than that it was just strange. We just felt strange vibes the night we heard the guy's voice."

The staff at the radio station then proceeded to listen to the tape of the show. The one general observation everybody, including the engineers, made, was that the voice quality was especially good. They slowed down the tape and listened. They could hear the last letter of every word he said. If he said "but," they could hear the "t" perfectly. "Generally on a telephone you can't hear those sounds at the end of the word. They just trail off," Mr. Smithers informed me. "It almost sounded to us like a voice-activated communications microphone. In other words, the pilot will have a small microphone inside a helmet and it is a mere inch away from his lips. You'll hear every single syllable in all he says. That's the kind of sound tape we had."

I asked Mr. Smithers to describe the incident. "One of the things that struck us and made our hair stand up a little was the first thing out of his mouth: 'There is one of you on the program tonight who will understand what I'm about to say.' The caller went on to explain that every living thing has an aura, and Page Bryant said, 'Yes, I agree.' Then he said the area you are talking about is the aura of the earth. He then said that it is the area through which the millionth council governs your planet. Then Allen Moore said, 'Did you say millionth?' Now we were trying to determine whether he meant million as a number or millenium. I don't think we ever did determine that because Allen said, 'millionth?' and the caller just repeated the word —'millionth.' The voice went on to say that when people are lost in the Triangle it is because some sort of communicative channel has been opened between the millionth council and the planet earth. He said the people who are gone are not dead, they are simply in a timeless void and happened to be at the wrong place at the wrong time, evidently. That basically was what he said, and in a nutshell hung up without a goodbye or a farewell."

Mr. Smithers said that his final conclusion is that "something strange is happening. I don't think that every case of people disappearing in the Triangle is mysterious. We're talking about eight and nine miles depth, so if a plane or a boat goes down in that kind of water of course there's not going to be debris. We're talking about the Gulf Stream that moves at about thirty-five miles an hour, so that a piece of wreckage can disappear from the area in a matter of hours and be up in West Virginia somewhere. By the same token, there are cases that are totally, absolutely, baffling and unexplainable. I think the most exciting angle is that of time-warps. There have been really well-substantiated cases of time-warps. It's just totally unexplainable. The thing that interests me the most, too, is that there have been millions of dollars worth of cargo gone. Government planes and ships have disappeared under mysterious conditions. Despite that, there have been no scientific efforts to find out if anything strange is happening."

According to Dr. Manson Valentine, an expert in magnetic disturbances, no one has taken magnetometers and crossed them in parallel points in order to measure magnetic fields in the Triangle.

Twenty-three-year-old pilot Bob Spielman has owned his own plane for eight years and frequently flies in the area of the Bermuda Triangle. One of the aircraft he owned for some time was a Beachcraft Bonanza, which is considered one of the finest and structurally strongest built planes on the market. Quite often he loaned it to friends who were also highly qualified pilots.

The day prior to his friends' accident Mr. Spielman flew his Bonanza into the same Triangle area with no incident. There was questionable weather but nothing uncommon to an experienced pilot. The following morning he loaned the plane to some friends who had flown it extensively. They flew in the area of the Grand Bahama Island on the way to a further destination.

They were in radio contact with the Miami Radio Aviation Facility when suddenly contact was lost. The plane never arrived at its destination.

The FAA put out an immediate search, and the wreckage was found some time later, all lives lost.

The following day Mr. Spielman went to the scene of the accident and went through the wreckage very carefully. Some parts of the aircraft were taken back to the Metallurgical Laboratory in Washington, D.C., for further examination. They found through extensive investigation that one of the main wing structures that held the wing in place had been subjected to such a terrific force that it wrenched the wing right off the airplane. The investigators found it unbelievable that such a force could exist.

The wing was found on a beach, while the main part of the wreckage was found approximately a quarter of a mile inland.

The weather that day was the finest possible for flying, with ceiling visibility unlimited.

Because of the way the disaster took place, the investigators found it difficult to believe that anyone could subject the aircraft to such a maneuver. The damage was done to only one part of the aircraft—the wing structure—whereas everything else was relatively intact. It was as though some strange force had attacked the wing area and wrenched it completely off the airplane.

Radio communications or electronically motivated instrumentation have often been affected and mysteriously lost in the Triangle and chalked up to experience, but when Mr. Spielman has returned from these occasions and carefully checked all the gadgetry aboard the aircraft, he has found them in working order, and wonders why atmospheric conditions didn't explain the temporary failure. He says, "Mechanical failure didn't explain it, it just happened."

15
Mediums and Mediumship and the Strange Case of Uri Geller

Many people connect the idea of a medium with the often-distorted image of the professional Spiritualist, who gets your uncle Joe "on the line" for a fee and who is sometimes a fake.

In the first place, *any* person who has had a number of psychic experiences of any kind is a medium or is mediumistic. One person in ten has this gift, in varying degrees, and potentially every one of us does. It is not supernatural or mystical. It is part of the human personality, merely a special extension of the senses or sensitivities, in the same way that some people are pianists or painters, and others are not.

Among the so-called *phases* of psychic ability there are two distinct groups. By "phase" I mean the particular *form* in which the ability to break through the time and space barrier manifests itself in you. It is possible to have several of these phases simultaneously. It is also possible to have just one. You can't jump from one to the other, if you are not so inclined, and if you force it, you will not succeed. Apparently, nature has a way of utilizing certain body conditions that lend themselves to certain specific forms of psychic ability.

The two big dividers are mental mediumship and physical mediumship. Perhaps I should explain the word *medium*. It isn't what Gian Carlo Menotti, author of the opera *The Medium,* made us believe—that a medium is a somewhat suspicious-looking individual, usually fat, who deals in communications with the dead.

Medium merely means intermediary, channel, and nothing else. A medium is simply a person who is able to create a *link* between the physical world and the other, nonphysical dimension. It can be a man or woman. It so happens that mediums are generally women because women are nearer to the emotional level required. Women, by and large, will also accept these truths more readily than will men, who tend to shy away from anything unorthodox that might put them into a special light with friends, neighbors, and business contacts. For every psychic individual of the male sex there are at least two of the female sex. The gift appears in children as well; in fact, it occurs with great frequency in very young children, then disappears at age four or five. Sometimes it returns in the late teens.

Mental mediumship, or the ability to receive information that cannot be accounted for by orthodox explanations, is by far the most common. It includes three different forms of perception: clairaudience, clairvoyance, and clairsentience. Clairaudience means to hear clearly; clairvoyance means to see clearly; clairsentience means to smell clearly. By far the largest percentage of people who have psychic abilities and psychic experiences *hear* something that they couldn't possibly hear under normal conditions. They might hear the voice of someone who is not present, or it might be an impression upon the unconscious, as if they heard some words, but whatever it is, it is auditory.

The clairvoyant sees, instead, an apparition, or a vision, or such phenomena as a symbol of some sort, before his mind's eye or even objectively outside himself.

A significantly smaller number of people have clairsentience, or the ability to smell something that isn't indicated by odors in the vicinity. The smell would be connected to some experience or tied in with another person, or it could be the perfume of a loved one who has passed on.

The other kind of mediumship, called *physical* mediumship, is far rarer and more complicated, and, in a way, holds a little danger at times. Physical means that the body of the person (the medium) is temporarily used by another entity. This applies equally to those who wish to be professional mediums and to ordinary people who have this ability and would like to control it. Those who have "dissociation of personality," the ability to slip out of their own physical bodies at intervals and sit, so to speak, next to themselves to allow someone else to operate their bodies temporarily, are called *physical mediums*. In *trance mediumship* the individual is unconscious, there is almost no heartbeat, and almost no pulse beat for a short moment before another person takes over the body.

There are people who lost a loved one and feel that by sitting or meeting with a medium the loved one will appear and say, "Well, Frances, things are all right. How are things with you?" But the dead seek out the living, the living cannot seek out the dead. If it is to your benefit to have this contact, it will come to you unsought at the proper time. Too, there are people who want to meet a medium because somebody has left them money and they can't find it or the papers proving it. Then there are missing persons. The late Florence Sternfels of New Jersey was called in at times by the police and has found a number of people, either dead or alive. It is a special kind of mediumship, taking a piece of cloth or a shoe belonging to the missing person and then reliving the scene of that person's last moments.

A lot of people think they have found the answer to the world's problems in a little piece of wood that they move around a ouiji board. They place their hands on it and all kinds of things happen. About ninety percent of these so-called communications are in the garbled unconscious of the sitters themselves; perhaps ten percent of the material is genuine.

Table tipping—similar to the ouija board—involves spelling out letters by the movement of a table.

The most controversial form of physical mediumship is *materialization*. This is the ability to bring into objective reality three-dimensional human figures. From the physical medium, as well as from the other "sitters," a physical substance is drawn from the glands of the human body. This is called ectoplasm. Tested in laboratories, it has been found to be a gray or whitish albumen substance. It can differ in density from smokelike to solid. Those who have touched it say it is "clammy and cold."

Materializations are the most desirable form of mediumship, for what is more exciting than to see your uncle Joe step out of a dark cabinet and shake hands with you. Consequently, it is much faked. But nothing is ever faked that doesn't also have a basis in fact. A very reputable, skeptical businessman of my acquaintance sat with the late Welsh psychic Jack Harris, who had a reputation as a materialization medium. Several others were present in a dark room, illuminated only by red light. Evidently, white or yellow-white light destroys the delicate tissues of ectoplasm, since they vibrate or move at the same rate of speed as light does. But red light, since it has a slower rate of vibration, does not interfere with it.

Harris was deeply entranced in his chair. Out of the floor rose several figures, building up slowly. They were at first nothing more than formless, whitish matter, gradually taking on the shapes of men or women until they would fill themselves out to be complete human beings. The sitters would shake hands with these entities. They would talk to them. After ten or fifteen minutes the entities would announce, "I have to go now, the power is running out" or something to that effect. And *in full view of everyone,* they would slowly become smaller and eventually melt into the floor whence they had come. This you cannot fake.

There are, however, in this country a number of such alleged mediums operating out of Spiritualist camps. These camps have some fine mental mediums in residence, but materializations are another matter. The telltale mark of fraudulent materialization is always the way the "spirits" come and go. If they simply disappear, quick as a flash, or come as quick as a flash, just stepping out, they usually are fraudulent. The real thing materializes slowly right before your eyes, from the floor, and disappears into the floor again.

Some people have trance mediumship when they don't seek it and at times when they don't want it. They simply slip into trances and are terrified at the prospect of doing so at the wrong time. This, too, can be rigidly controlled, by understanding the problem and by firmly applying self-discipline.

If you believe that your door to perception is closed, then it is. The individual's attitude is important, and often trance mediums are burdened with emotional maladjustment, which does not allow them full control over such emotion-tinged phenomena as onsetting trances. Such individuals can be helped through hypnotherapy to gain full control over their faculties of this nature, either to suppress them, if this is absolutely necessary for reasons of health, or to develop them and channel the power into useful areas, where it can be controlled and observed.

Trance is *not* hypnosis. Hypnosis is often used to induce trance states, but it is only a tool to open the door to the unconscious more effectively or more quickly. Hypnosis is a state in which suggestions can be implanted. Trance is the very opposite. Here the researcher gets information from the subject.

There are few good trance mediums capable of total "dissociation of personality"—that is, able to completely get out of their own physical body, sit by their side, so to speak, and let someone else use their body for a while without interposing any part of their own personality.

We know far too little about the biochemical makeup of the human body to reject arbitrarily the notion of ectoplasm. The substance was, in fact, isolated some years ago and examined chemically. It was then found to be an albumen-rich substance, and definitely of material found in living beings. How it gets out of the body without being seen by the observers, and how it is rapidly or instantaneously shaped into a figure or part of a figure, is not fully understood. But does the body not send forth the equally invisible sweat from its sweat glands under emotional or physical stress? Perhaps the ectoplastic emanations work similarly when the right psychic conditions prevail.

Some mediums don't want to let go of their "trade" even after they themselves have gone to the other side.

Hans Holzer reported an astounding incident concerning a medium he had worked with, Florence Sternfels.

> On May 19, 1965, I conducted an investigation of a reputedly haunted house at Ringwood, New Jersey, which is not very far from Edgewater. My medium on that occasion was Ethel Johnson Meyers, and we were also accompanied by my wife, Catherine, and Haskel Frankel, an editor of the *Saturday Review* at that time and later Senior Editor on the *Saturday Evening Post*.
>
> We had hardly entered the Ringwood manor house and seated ourselves at a huge round dining room table when Ethel fell into deep trance. Expecting a voice from the past of this historically very active mansion, I was startled when a strongly familiar sound came from Ethel Meyer's entranced lips.
>
> "Mr. Holzer . . . hello . . . oh, Mr. Holzer!" The voice spoke out loud. "Hello!"
>
> "Who is it?" I asked.
>
> "Don't you recognize Florence?" the voice reprimanded me. "I'm so glad to talk to you." It was the exact tone of voice that had always been characteristic of a telephone call from Florence! No mistaking it—this *was* Florence speaking.
>
> "You passed over two weeks ago, Florence," I said gently.
>
> "I just want to say hello."
>
> "How did you find me here?" I wondered out loud.
>
> "Well, I've been watching for a long time . . . I wanted to call you but I can never get you on the phone . . . I don't know why, but here you are!"

According to Denis Brian, the celebrated Jeane Dixon has a "God-given gift of prophecy." She accurately predicted that President Kennedy and his brother Robert would be killed. In fact, many of her predictions involve the deaths of famous persons.

Jeane Dixon says that although the death of John Kennedy was inevitable, the deaths of Robert Kennedy, Martin Luther King, and others could have been prevented. She claims that some of her most powerful vibrations were intended to help the Kennedy family and eventually the world—but that the Kennedys rejected her warnings.

"The plane is going to crash," Jeane Dixon told her husband shortly after she was married. She begged him to make his business trip from Detroit to Chicago by train. He told his wife that this trip was too important and he didn't want to be late for the meeting.

It doesn't take a skeptic to reject this incident with very little evidence and no documentation to authenticate it. But would the plane crash or did her "gift of prophecy" have a purpose other than to scare?

When her husband, James Dixon, decided at the last moment not to fly to Chicago, another man was standing in line to have his ticket checked. He heard Dixon say he wasn't going to fly, and he too decided to go by train.

The plane did crash, killing all passengers on board.

Ethel Johnson Meyers was a trained singer in her native San Francisco. Later she worked as a singer in vaudeville. She had no interest in or involvement with psychic research or mediumship until much later in life. She discovered her ability accidentally, after the death of her first husband. Despondent over his passing, she was considering suicide when he materialized to her and prevented her from taking her own life. Since that time she has become more and more involved in the psychic, developing herself as a medium and studying the phenomena at the same time. Mrs. Meyers is both a trance medium and a clairvoyant.

Jimmie Jacobs, who makes his living producing strip shows in London, was also a Spiritualist and a very talented amateur medium. Every year he made predictions concerning the future of the world, which were published in the daily press. He did so not to seek notoriety, but out of a genuine sense of psychic mission: he felt that he must contribute toward a better understanding of extrasensory perception. Over the years, Mr. Jacobs has scored quite high. More than half of his predictions came true.

Sybil Leek is probably best known as a witch, but not many people realize that she was a writer and documentary producer for many years in England and that she has made her mark in many other fields. Her belief in the "old religion"—the ancient Celtic faith commonly called Wicca, or witchcraft—is part of her private life. The fact that she is a great trance medium is in no way related to this belief.

Sybil Leek functions on many levels. She is a businesswoman, a journalist, a writer of books. She is also the mother of two grown sons, Julian and Stephen— one a talented photographer and designer, the other a television cameraman. Mrs Leek does not give or seek private readings as professional mediums do. Occasionally she does so as part of promotion for her books. Since so much of what she has said in the past seems significant, one must respect her psychic abilities. She also works as a professional astrologer, but Mrs. Leek does not confuse the two crafts. As an astrologer she forecasts trends mathematically, but as a psychic she predicts them.

Many individuals are convinced of an afterlife because of peculiar experiences, I discovered, experiences that they had when they were or thought themselves to be near death.

Lori Moore was severely injured by a train in 1960; her spinal cord was ruptured. After undergoing major surgery, she was put in intensive care, where a nurse found her in shock. "I was in great pain and slowly I drifted into what I thought was sleep. But then I realized that I was aware of the room and my perspective was from the ceiling down. I saw a nurse enter the room. She looked at my body, shook it hard several times, and then ran out." A few nurses and two doctors entered the room with equipment and connected wires to Lori's body. She saw them working over her and clearly heard their voices. She also heard another voice. "You've been suffering a long time. You can come this way, or you can go back." The voice came from no specific direction or person, and it was neither male nor female in tone; "like a voice I have never heard," says Lori.

The voice spoke for a while, telling her that if she went back there would be much suffering and pain ahead from the injury. "I wanted to go. The feelings were so pleasant, there was no pain, no fear. And yet I felt a tugging back, something drawing me to my body."

At this point images of her three children appeared (ages four, five, and seven). They said nothing and the voice did not mention them, but Lori knew that she was being given a chance to make a choice. "I was just a step away from going, it would have been so easy to take that next step, but the images of the children stopped me. I couldn't leave them. I actually felt them tugging on my soul." All the while Lori had full awareness of the actions and words of the doctors and nurses, and she remembered these things.

She drifted down from the ceiling and reentered her body. She feels that this was a willful act on her part, that it was not the medical techniques that saved her; she did not have to return if she did not want to. Later, in the hospital, she told her husband about the experience. "He said it was just a nightmare, but I knew that it was no hallucination. . . . I became friendly with one of the nurses who saw me every day. Eventually I told her of the experience and of the dialogue that I had heard during the operation to revive me." The nurse confirmed the facts that Lori had no blood pressure and heartbeat—in fact, that she had lost all vital life signs—and also confirmed all the things that Lori had heard the doctors and nurses discussing over her body.

"I was in the hospital for several weeks after the experience, and in great pain the whole time. The only thing that gave me strength was the experience, it made me a more spiritual person."

Eventually Lori told her doctor about the experience. She claims that it upset him greatly, because she knew so much of what had taken place when she was supposed to have been totally unconscious. "He became very silent, turned his chair around, and stared out the window for a long time. He said, 'Don't tell me any more. I thought you were gone.'"

The experience changed Lori's life. She entered nursing school and graduated in 1974. Currently she is working for the Center for Living with Dying, in San Jose; she and other professionals attempt to teach people who are terminally ill to cope with death, especially not to fear it.

Lori appeared on a panel recently at J.F.K. University and told of her experience. She has received some criticism from doctors for making her experience public. One doctor said, "You're a nurse, dedicated to helping people recover and live. It is not appropriate that a nurse talk about an afterlife." At first Lori was surprised at the negative feedback, but now she believes that there are some doctors who want to believe that a dying (or clinically dead) person cannot make his own choice about returning to life. If a clinically dead person is resuscitated, it is because of the "efforts of the medical team"!

Lori's husband now looks on her experience with different eyes. He believes it was a religious encounter and that it has changed their lives. A few weeks ago, Lori was critically ill with bleeding ulcers. "I almost died, but I can honestly say that I had absolutely no fear of death." Lori and her husband talk openly about her out-of-the-body experience, and she has become much more comfortable with it now that she realizes that thousands of other people have experienced the same thing.

Sheldon Ruderman has had two near-death experiences, one seven and the other sixteen years ago. The first OBE (out-of-body experience) occurred after an eight-hour operation to remove a cancerous right lung. Sheldon found that he was not able to regain full consciousness from the medication he had been given. "I struggled for a while, trying to open my eyes and shout for a nurse, but I seemed to have absolutely no control over my body. Then suddenly I had no sense of breathing; I was completely paralyzed. I must be dead, I thought. I saw a veiled light, hazy, I could see no shapes or forms and then I was out of my body, floating over the bed. I thought, well, this is what it is like to be dead. I knew that I was dead and I was relieved that it was all over." The scientific side of Sheldon emerged during his OBE. "I felt like an anthropologist visiting the land of the dead." He studied the room, his body on the bed, and was very analytical in his observations. He was never afraid, and maintained a sense of humor throughout the experience. Abruptly he found himself back in his body, with a doctor standing at his bedside.

Years later, he had another chest operation. His medical condition was so bad that the doctors could not give him a general anesthetic; he had only an injection of Novocain and was awake during the entire operation. "Medical students were present and they stood around the table. The doctor broke my ribs to get into my chest. It did not hurt; it felt as though a hammer covered in a thick fabric tapped against my bones. However, the idea of lying on the table with my chest cut open and only on an injection of Novocain worried me; I kept thinking I might suddenly feel the whole thing. I wanted to see what the doctors were doing." Sheldon's desire to see the operation was realized by an OBE. "First I imagined a diving board extending over the operating table and tried to picture what the view would be like from the board. The next thing I knew I was actually lying on the board, looking down at my own surgery. I could see the people clearly, but my body was slightly blurred. The opening in my chest was even more blurred. Occasionally the doctor would ask me how I felt. I could not answer him from up on the diving board. I had to go back into my body, tell him I was fine, then float up to the board again. When I was out I had no sensation of the doctor cutting or breaking bones."

Sheldon did not tell anyone about his experiences until recently, when he learned of other people telling similar stories. "I was an atheist, and I came to these experiences very scientific and analytical in my reasoning. But when you go through experiences like these, and it's not part of your cultural repertoire, you at first think you're going crazy. But when I compare notes with others who have had experiences like mine, the similarities are too striking; the experiences are real enough."

Sheldon now feels that man has two bodies, a physical one plus one that has no tissues, no bones, and no awareness of pain. Recently Sheldon had another OBE, and it convinced him that there is such a thing as a cosmic consciousness; that the astral body belongs to this cosmic entity.

As with virtually everyone who has had a near-death experience, it changed Sheldon's life. He left engineering and is now a clinical psychologist (though he also refers to himself as a social scientist), counseling dying cancer patients. He has had many patients tell him stories like his own. "You begin to realize that OBEs are not rare, thousands of people have them. It's just that before now people were afraid to tell anyone about them."

Claudette L. Kiely is a teacher and mother. She is also a gifted psychic who has done some impressive work with Dr. Karlis Osis at the American Society for Psychical Research in New York. Claudette has had one near-death experience (during the birth of her third child) and many OBEs—she can induce them at will and travel great distances.

After the normal delivery in 1962 of her third child, a girl, Claudette experienced great difficulty discharging the placenta. Problems developed on the delivery table and at one point Claudette found herself floating out of her body. She saw a tunnel with a beautiful white light at the end. She knew that she had to get to that light. But a voice was speaking to her. It was a friendly voice that was neither male nor female. It kept telling her: "Remember the children. They need you. What about the new baby?" The voice grew more desperate, and soon she went into a "reverse tumbling action." She reentered her body and the placenta was discharged. The doctor later questioned her on what, if anything, she had experienced on the table. Claudette claimed that something had happened (she felt that she had died), but the doctor would never give her any information on the details.

A few years ago she took part in Dr. Osis's "fly-ins" —attempts to have people from around the country fly in with their astral bodies to the laboratory at the ASPR and discern target items. Claudette was able to do this; in one experiment she identified a bird that was on a table and gave the exact layout of the room—all while her physical body was in Massachusetts. She (and Dr.

Osis) tell of an interesting event: One evening when she flew in, a research associate at ASPR saw a blue mist in the target room. It moved around the table and over to the fireplace. A telephone call later confirmed that at the time the mist appeared in the room, Claudette was engaged in an OBE traveling to the target room and viewing the objects. It was ten o'clock at night and she was at her home in Grandy, Mass., wearing a *blue* bathrobe.

Claudette also tells of just how she separates her astral and physical bodies—up through the head—and how one time she got stuck "trying to get out." As she describes it, her big astral feet got stuck in her physical head.

Some psychics have done impressive laboratory work for scientists. Alex Tanous, who holds a Ph.D. in theology and is a psychic, has been tested in many laboratories. Recently Dr. Tanous worked with Dr. Karlis Osis at the American Society for Psychical Research in New York City. Tanous voluntarily had OBE and was able to travel to "target rooms" and perceive objects, and apparently caused a feather to move with his astral body. During all these experiments Dr. Tanous's physical body was locked in a Farraday Cage—a room shielded from electromagnetic (radio) waves. Tanous sees his astral body as a "ball of light"; it is small, and it is the ball that travels to various locations. At one time Osis requested Tanous to "see" into an optical box and report the image. Tanous tried and failed. The box was too high; his light ball could not look into it. A platform was built a few inches below the glass window of the box, and from that time on Tanous's astral body was able to go to the platform and see into the box.

Because Tanous believed his astral body was a ball of light, Osis decided to see if sensitive equipment could detect the light. An experiment was set up at the New York headquarters of the Energy Research Group, headed by Dr. Richard Dobrin, a physicist. The ERG has extremely sensitive light-detection equipment (in fact, they have designed a "black room"—one that is virtually free of all visible radiation). Targets were put in the "black room" and Tanous was locked in a men's room down the hall. Not only was he able to travel to the room and perceive the targets correctly, but the light-detection equipment actually measured a "presence" or "bursts of light" in the room.

During one experiment at the ASPR, Tanous was in Maine. When he "flew in" to "see" the target objects in New York, psychic Christine Whiting, who was at the ASPR and in the target room, reported actually seeing Tanous's astral body (psychics throughout history have claimed to be able to see the astral body). Whiting's observation and Tanous's time of fly-in corresponded perfectly.

Stuart "Blue" Harary is of Egypto-Syrian-Jewish parentage and is also a psychic who has been extensively studied by several scientists. He is now at the Psychical Research Foundation, Durham, N.C., undergoing some pretty novel OBE experiments under the direction of research director Dr. William Roll.

The premise of the Psychical Research Foundation's work with Blue is quite simple but very novel: Parapsychological literature is full of references to the psychical sensitivity of animals, especially cats, who have served as companions and seers for witches centuries. Dr. Roll was convinced that Blue had OBEs at will, as he had been tested for this many times with success. Additionally, Dr. Roll wanted to see if the astral body could be detected—not by scientific equipment, as Dr. Osis had done, but by use of animals: cats and snakes were chosen in this experiment, designed by Dr. Robert Morris.

A young kitten was obtained for Blue. He raised it for a while, fed it, and attempted to develop a genuine rapport with the cat so that it was well aware of who he was. In the experiment, Blue's pet kitten was placed on an activity board that was shaped like a shuffleboard and marked off into many squares; they determined the cat's activity by counting how many squares it moved during the experiment. Comparisons were to be made between the cat's activity when Blue was undergoing an astral projection into the box containing the checkerboard and when Blue was not projecting. The experiment worked beautifully. During control periods (when

Blue was not projecting) the cat was rambunctious, tried to escape from the box, rushed about, and vocalized profusely. However, when Blue was "present," the cat became very passive, sat motionless, and did not vocalize; during these periods the cat behaved exactly like it did in Blue's physical presence. The statistical difference between the activity of the kitten during the control and experimental times was less than one in 100 that the result was due to mere chance.

Since the cat seemed to prefer different sections of the box at different times when Blue was projecting, the PRF scientists thought that the cat could actually localize Blue's presence. A new experiment was set up. The cat was placed in a large room and its behavior was monitored by closed-circuit TV cameras. Blue, in another room, had to project to randomly selected sections of the target room. Hopefully, the cat would go to the corner of the room where Blue astrally positioned himself. Mild results were obtained. At times the cat did go to the exact location that Blue was in. However, a surprise occurred. Dr. John Hartwell, the psychophysiologist monitoring the test, began having weird impressions as to where and when Blue was present. In fact, Hartwell became very successful at "guessing" when Blue was present. Once he not only correctly determined that Blue was present but actually saw his apparition over the monitor.

Psychophysiological readings were also taken on Blue during his projections; they showed differences in respiration, an increase in heart rate, a decrease in skin electrical potential, an increase in blood pulse volume, but little brainwave (EEG) change.

If Blue could have a calming effect on his kitten with the presence of his astral body, what would happen if he projected himself into a glass terrarium containing a snake? Blue and Dr. Morris were in one building; the snake was in another building, with psychical researcher Dr. Scot Rogo, who was to monitor the snake's behavior. Dr. Rogo, of course, had no idea at what times Blue would attempt projections. At one point the snake made some pretty violent moves (having been motionless prior to this). It quickly ascended the side of the glass, bit and gnawed at it, and came back to the ground and was noticeably excited. When notes and times were compared, it was found that the snake's strange activity correlated perfectly with Blue's projection into the terrarium.

In addition to the animal research experiments, Dr. Roll has been testing Blue's ability to hear music with his astral body. Selections of various pieces are randomly played in one room while Blue, a quarter of a mile away, projects into the room, and identifies the music upon bodily return.

Blue claims that he has been able to have OBEs since early childhood. For many years he did not tell anyone about them for fear of being thought crazy. A few years ago he heard of the OBE work being done by Osis at the ASPR and became part of that work—he had amazing success in the area of fly-ins. OBEs hold no religious overtones for him; they are simple experiences that he believes many people have, or could have if they knew what to do. He has his own ideas of how to bring on an OBE.

Robert Monroe is a businessman and psychic noted for his OBE work. He was first known for the OBE work done on him in the late 1960s by Dr. Charles Tart, at the University of California. Mr. Monroe has since opened the Monroe Institute, where he has been teaching psychiatrists and psychologists how to have OBEs.

Monroe spontaneously began to have OBEs in 1958 and since then he's been "out" thousands of times. He kept a detailed log of his OBEs and published them in 1971 in a book titled *Journeys Out of the Body*. In August 1966 Tart had eight sessions with Monroe, in which brainwaves, eye movements, and heart rate were electronically monitored while Monroe tried to travel out of his body and read a five-digit number that was on a shelf in an adjacent room. He could never read the number, but twice when he said he was "out" he gave Tart descriptions of activities that were taking place in other parts of the building. Tart checked these out and Monroe was proved correct. Tart found that Monroe's brainwave patterns were typical to those of dreaming.

In the summer of 1968 Tart worked with Monroe again. Once again Monroe could not read the target numbers, but he did provide correct information of events outside the lab. During Monroe's wanderings out of his body, Tart observed definite physiological correlates. Monroe's blood pressure dropped, his eye movements increased, and his brainwave pattern switched to prolonged theta rhythms typical of the "twilight" period between wakefulness and sleep.

Prospective students (fifty percent are Ph.D.s and M.D.s) for the Monroe Institute are put through a rigorous psychological screening process. Out of approximately six hundred who pass this level, about fifty emerge as really "proficient" OBE practitioners, six actually gifted. A typical trainee begins with a rigorous weekend session. The program includes yoga breathing exercises, visualization techniques, and the use of an "audio pulsing device."

This device has been patented by Monroe, and, he claims, is used in university sleep research throughout the country. The instrument produces sounds that have the exact same pulsating rhythms as the brain's own sleep waves. As a person falls to sleep, his brain waves pass from wakeful beta waves (thirty to thirteen cycles per second) to the slower alpha waves (twelve to eight cps) characteristic of mild meditative states, to theta waves (seven to three cps), to delta waves (three to one cps). Monroe's device produces sounds that run through these waves in just the order and amount that is experienced in falling asleep naturally. But Monroe is not, of course, interested in putting his subjects to sleep. Instead, using the audio pulsing device, he "suspends" his subjects between theta and delta levels. In other words, he locks subjects in at the very threshold of deep sleep, but not sleep. This level of consciousness, Monroe believes (as do other researchers), is conducive to OBEs. Monroe says his device is used regularly at the Veterans' Administration Hospital in his area for sleep research.

Subjects have OBEs, travel to near and distant locations, and report back on their sightings and on the nature of their experiences. Many psychologists and psychiatrists have taken Monroe's course for the experience of being out of one's body. In this state, a person can be free of the physical shell, open to a free flow of imagery, strange voices, transcending space and time, viewing events that happened in the past—all these things, claims Monroe, greatly help therapists treat psychotics and other mentally disturbed people. The OBE, says Monroe, gives the psychiatrist some "feeling" for another-world type of existence, and permits him to better appreciate the "imaginary" voices, images, and experiences that are common to people who are considered mentally disturbed. Monroe says that some of his subjects report that they have been able to "reach" their own patients and help them make contacts with reality since the *therapists themselves* have had a glimpse of an alternate reality.

Ingo Swann is a New York City psychic who has worked with many scientists on the east and west coasts. He is also a professional artist who does paintings of OBEs. "I do not try to portray what I see and feel during an OBE," he said, "but I try to create a painting that will let the viewer vicariously have the sensations I have during my OBE travel." Swann claims he always had an awareness that his spirit was not confined to his physical body.

He views OBEs differently from other psychics. Where they claim that the spirit is an astral body often with the same shape as the physical body, Swann says that an OBE is merely an extension through space and time of one's consciousness. Instead of an OBE being a projection of the astral body, says Swann, it is a willful projection of a fluidlike consciousness. Interestingly, he says that it is not a special talent, but a natural function of human consciousness and thus something that every person can achieve.

Why then do relatively few people report the ability to have OBEs? They don't, says Swann. At least they don't lack the talent to have an OBE, but, due to conditioning, Western schooling in the sciences of the body, and the belief that extensions of human consciousness are impossible, most people never try to have OBEs. "If they would only believe that it was possible for them, and try it," says Swann, "they would be amazed how easily they could have the OBE." Swann blames our Western culture for suffocating psychic talents in people.

He says that he can control his astral travels to a large degree—that is, he can select a specific location and go to it. He can also be given the latitude and longitude coordinates of a place he has never visited before and can project himself there and, with remarkable accuracy, give a detailed description of the place. He has done this for several scientists, especially Dr. Karlis Osis of the American Society for Psychical Research in New York City, and Drs. Harold Puthoff and Russell Tart at Stanford Research Institute, Menlo Park, California.

I asked Swann about possession. Can a discarnate spirit in the vicinity of a person undergoing an OBE enter that person's body? Swann thinks this is not likely. It is possible, but he has never considered it. He sees possession more likely in the mentally disturbed than in the psychic. Not everyone agrees with this, of course. He says that if possession was really possible then we should see more cases of it in people who have OBEs. But we do not, he claims.

How does Swann prepare for an OBE? He does not. Unlike most psychics and others who have OBEs, Swann has no special breathing exercises, postures, mental images—nothing. He merely decides consciously that he is going to have an OBE, selects the location he wishes to visit (often determined by the scientists studying him), and goes.

In the last five years, because he has had so many OBEs for scientists on the east and west coasts, he claims his proficiency has greatly increased. He has them more easily, can control his travels much better, and can obtain more evidential material from the target location. Practice, he says, is just as important in perfecting astral travel as in any endeavor.

Swann is a psychic loved by scientists, for he is more interested in being studied than in giving stage performances of his powers, as Uri Geller does.

The following scientists have worked closely with near-death persons and those psychics and ordinary individuals who have OBEs.

Dr. Karlis Osis, director of research, American Society for Psychical Research, has been working on OBE research for years. In 1971 he was awarded $300,000 from the James Kidd will for research on proof of an astral body or soul. Most of the money was to be spent recording deathbed observations in the U.S. and India. Some of the money was also used in the OBE fly-in type experiments and the work with Alex Tanous.

The ASPR study has been completed. Dr. Osis surveyed 1,004 physicians and nurses in the U.S. and 704 in India. Many were interviewed in depth about their dying patients' last few hours. "Dying patients insist that they have glimpses of postmortem existence," said Osis. "They see persons long dead, scenes of otherworldly beauty, and they have out-of-body experiences." Here are some findings: in two thirds of the cases where people saw apparitions, the apparition wanted to take the dying person away to another level of existence. The apparitions "called," "beckoned," and some even "demanded" the dying person to come to them. According to medical factors such as brain damage, high fever, uremic poisoning, and heavy medication, Dr. Osis showed that the apparitions were not likely to be explained away as mere hallucinations—most of the people who reported them were fully coherent up until the moment of death. Nor were the apparitions of "take-away figures," as Dr. Osis calls them, mere "wish fulfillment" on the part of the dying person, because in many cases the person did not want to go with the apparition and screamed for help or asked the doctor to protect or hide him. During OBEs the dying often saw a light and heard a voice, just as did the near-death individuals.

Dr. Charles Tart, professor of psychology at the University of California, did the highly regarded work with Robert Monroe. Dr. Tart is a well-informed, well-spoken, leading scientist in the field of OBEs.

Dr. Raymond A. Moody, Jr., a Ph.D. in philosophy,

received his M.D. recently and should soon begin residency in psychiatry at the University of Virginia School of Medicine.

Over the past five years Moody has personally interviewed more than one hundred persons who have experienced "clinical death" and been revived. He has put his findings together in a recently published book, *Life After Life*.

Moody divides his many cases into two main categories: (1) the experiences of persons who were resuscitated after having been thought, or pronounced, clinically dead by their doctors; (2) the experiences of persons who, in the course of accidents or severe injury or illness, came very close to physical death. He has interviewed some fifty persons in great detail. He finds the following similarities:

Ineffability: "There are just no words to express what I am trying to say," says the typical near-death person. Or, "They just don't make adjectives and superlatives to describe this." One woman explained it to Dr. Moody this way:

> "There is a real problem for me as I'm trying to tell you this, because all the words I know are three-dimensional. As I was going through this, I kept thinking, 'Well, when I was taking geometry they always told me there were only three dimensions. But they are wrong. There are more.' . . . And that's why it's so hard to tell you this. I have to describe it to you in words that are three-dimensional. That's as close as I can get to it, but it's not really adequate. I can't really give you a complete picture."

Feelings of peace and quiet: Many people, says Moody, report feelings of euphoria. Typical, he says, is this man's report after a severe head injury:

> "At the point of injury there was a momentary flash of pain, but then all the pain vanished. I had the feeling of floating in a dark space. The day was bitterly cold, yet while I was in that blackness all I felt was warmth and the most extreme comfort I have ever experienced."

Noise: Many people report hearing a buzzing sound, not music as we might think. Sometimes, says Moody, the noises are extremely unpleasant. It's been variously described as a "loud ring," a "whistling sound, like the wind," a "buzzing like a swarm of bees" and on the other hand like the "tinkling of Japanese bells," and like "soft beautiful music."

Dark tunnel: Often when the noise is present so too is a dark tunnel; the person feels he is in a tunnel, speeding along it. Typical is this report by a man so near death that his pupils dilated and his body began growing cold:

> "I was in an utterly black, dark void. It is very difficult to explain, but I felt as if I were moving in a vacuum, just through blackness. Yet, I was quite conscious. It was like being in a cylinder which had no air in it. It was a feeling of limbo, of being half-way here, and half-way somewhere else."

Meeting others: Many people during the near-death OBEs claim they meet long-dead persons (Dr. Osis's work in the U.S. and India strongly supports this). "They became aware of the presence of other spiritual beings in their vicinity," says Moody, "beings who apparently were there to ease them through their transition into death, or, in some cases, to tell them that their time to die had not yet come and that they must return to their physical bodies."

The Being of Light: "What is perhaps the most incredible common element in the accounts I have studied," says Moody, "and is certainly the element which has the most profound effect upon the individual, is the encounter with a very bright light. Typically, at first the light is dim, it grows brighter as the person approaches it, and eventually attains an unearthly brilliance." Yet, despite the extreme brightness, the light never hurts a person's eyes or makes him squint. The light often talks, and this is the voice that many people say is neither male nor female in its tone.

Another common element, says Moody, is that those persons who have near-death encounters lose their fear of death. "They have seen death and know that it is even more than life was. It is a continuing cycle, not an abrupt end."

Dr. Moody is a philosopher and he is extremely well-versed in the writings of Plato, the Bible, the Tibetan Book of the Dead, and various philosophers throughout history who have written about OBEs. Moody claims that references to an astral body and the ability to separate it from the physical body can be found in many staid philosophical works.

Dr. Pascal Kaplan is the dean of the School of General Studies, John F. Kennedy University, Orinda, California. He is fully versed in the whole field of OBEs and near-death encounters. In March of this year he organized and headed a "Professional Seminar" at JFK University on the subject of OBEs and dying.

Where many of the research scientists make very little of the possibility of possession during OBEs (some say it is impossible and unheard of), Dr. Kaplan is genuinely concerned about the possibility and he knows of a few cases where it is supposed to have happened.

Probably the most exciting new medium to burst upon the scene in recent times is young Israeli ex-paratrooper Uri Geller.

In 1971 Andrija Puharich met Uri Geller, whose psychic abilities had already made him well known in his homeland. The next year Uri came to America, where millions of people have since watched him bend keys, stop watches, and break metal rings, with no apparent physical pressure. So far no one has been able to explain how he does these things.

Dr. Puharich reported Uri's exploits, including some near-incredible contacts with outer-space intelligences.

The doctor's first experiment was to see if Uri had the power to move a magnetic compass needle solely by mental effort. Two liquid-filled compasses were used as test instruments. Since Uri had never before tried to move a compass needle, he was very unsure of himself. Before the tests began, Uri gave the doctor permission to search his body for any hidden devices; nothing was found.

After seven minutes of concentration, Uri was able to move a compass needle sixteen degrees clockwise.

On the second try, Uri asked the doctor to place some rubber bands on his left hand, which acted as a tourniquet, the better to occlude the venous return from his hand. The doctor agreed to do this since it could not compromise the test conditions. Uri was now able, with great mental effort, to move the compass needle ninety degrees clockwise.

In a series of telepathy tests, Uri received numbers, colors, and symbols from several people present. He was one-hundred-percent correct in twenty attempts.

One of the people present held a watch that was filmed before it was covered, and the hands read 9:25 P.M. Uri then placed his hand over the person's, without touching it. The person said she "felt a thin streak of energy going through my hand." The watch was examined in one minute; the hands now read 8:13 P.M. Under Uri's influence, the hands had moved back seventy-two minutes.

Then Dr. Puharich's watch, which had a stainless-steel spring watchband, was placed on a table. Uri asked that some pieces of metal knives, spoons, etc., be placed around it. Uri placed his left hand over the doctor's watch without touching it. He took his hand away in twenty seconds. The steel band of the watch was twisted where it joined the body of the watch. This was a most impressive feat.

Since then, Geller has astounded large audiences the world over with his mental bending and other teleki-netic efforts, at the same time arousing the ire of professional debunkers and magicians who insist it is all a trick.

According to the text of a report by the Stanford Research Institute, Geller presented a subject worthy of further study:

Here are a number of the spoons that were bent by one means or another during the course of our experiments. There is no doubt that the spoons were bent. The only doubt remains as to the manner of their bending. Similarly, we have rings that were bent by Mr. Geller. The rings that were bent are shown here. The copper ring at the left and the brass ring at the right were manufactured at SRI and measured to require 150 pounds of force to bend them. These rings were in Geller's hand at the time they were bent.

This brief recap is to remind you of those experiments we feel were best controlled. They are the three perception experiments, including drawings in envelopes, the double-blind hidden-object experiments, and the double-blind die-in-the-box experiment. The two psychokinetic experiments—the depression or raising of a weight on an electrical scale and the deflection of the magnetometer—also do not seem to admit of any ready counter-hypothesis.

BIBLIOGRAPHY

Berlitz, Charles. *The Berumda Triangle*. New York: Doubleday.

———. *Mysteries From Forgotten Worlds*. New York: Doubleday.

Brian, Denis and Dixon, Jeane. *The Witnesses*. New York: Doubleday.

Cranston, S. L. *Reincarnation*. New York: Julian Press.

Gould, R. T. *Enigmas*. Secaucus, New Jersey: University Press.

Grant, Joan and Kelsey, Denys. *Many Lifetimes*. New York: Doubleday.

Hogg, Gary. *Odd Aspects of England*. New York: Arco.

Holzer, Hans. *Beyond Medicine*. New York: Ballantine.

———. *Born Again*. New York: Doubleday.

———. *ESP and You*. New York: Ace.

———. *Ghost Hunter*. Indianapolis, Indiana: Bobbs-Merrill.

———. *The Ghost Hunter's Strangest Cases*. New York: Ace.

———. *The Handbook of Parapsychology*. New York: Manor.

———. *Haunted Houses*. New York: Crown.

———. *Life After Death: The Challenge and the Evidence*. Indianapolis, Indiana: Bobbs-Merrill.

———. *Patterns of Destiny*. Plainview, New York: Nash.

———. *The Prophets Speak*. New York: Manor.

———. *Psychic Photography: Threshold of a New Science?* New York: Drake.

———. *The Psychic Side of Dreams*. New York: Doubleday.

———. *The Psychic World of Plants*. New York: Pyramid.

Ostrander, Sheila and Schroeder, Lynn. *Psychic Discoveries Behind the Iron Curtain*. Englewood Cliffs, N. J.: Prentice-Hall.

Puharich, Andrija. *Uri*. New York: Doubleday.

Sherman, Harold. *"Wonder" Healers of the Philippines*. Psychic Press.

Tester, M. H. *The Healing Touch*. New York: Taplinger.

Tompkins, Peter. *The Secrets of the Great Pyramid*. New York: Harper & Row.

Umland, E. and C. *Mystery of the Ancients*. New York: Walker.

Underwood, Peter. *Gazetteer of British Ghosts*. New York: Walker.

Walker, E. D. *Reincarnation*. New York: University Books.

ABOUT THE AUTHOR

ALAN LANDSBURG is a successful film and television producer, heading up his own production company in Los Angeles, California. He was instrumental in bringing the von Däniken phenomenon to the attention of the American public through T.V. by producing "In Search of Ancient Astronauts." Alan Landsburg is also the author of *In Search of Ancient Mysteries* and *The Outer Space Connection*. He is currently working on a weekly television series, "In Search of . . .," which has been on the air since September, 1976. *In Search of Strange Phenomena* and five other books on extraterrestrials, monsters, lost civilizations, magic and witchcraft and people, are based on this series.

OTHER WORLDS
OTHER REALITIES

In fact and fiction, these extraordinary books bring the fascinating world of the supernatural down to earth from ancient astronauts and black magic to witchcraft, voodoo and mysticism—these books look at other worlds and examine other realities.

- [ ] **THE REINCARNATION OF PETER PROUD (6444/$1.75)—Fiction**
- [ ] **IN SEARCH OF ANCIENT MYSTERIES (8376/$1.50)—Fact**
- [ ] **THE DEVIL'S TRIANGLE (10688/$1.75)—Fact**
- [ ] **POWER THROUGH WITCHCRAFT (8673/$1.25)—Fact**
- [ ] **CHARIOTS OF THE GODS (Q5753/$1.25)—Fact**
- [ ] **A COMPLETE GUIDE TO THE TAROT (T2796/$1.50)—Fact**
- [ ] **GODS FROM OUTER SPACE (2466/$1.50)—Fact**
- [ ] **NOT OF THIS WORLD (7696/$1.25)—Fact**
- [ ] **GOD DRIVES A FLYING SAUCER (7733/$1.25)—Fact**
- [ ] **THE SPACESHIPS OF EZEKIEL (8378/$1.95)—Fact**
- [ ] **THE OUTER SPACE CONNECTION (2092/$1.75)—Fact**

Buy them at your local bookstore or use this handy coupon for ordering:

Bantam Books, Inc., Dept. OW, 414 East Golf Road, Des Plaines, Ill. 60016

Please send me the books I have checked above. I am enclosing $_____ (please add 35¢ to cover postage and handling). Send check or money order —no cash or C.O.D.'s please.

Mr/Mrs/Miss_____

Address_____

City_____State/Zip_____

OW—2/77

Please allow three weeks for delivery. This offer expires 2/78.

PSYCHIC WORLD

Here are some of the leading books that delve *the world of the occult—that shed light on the powers of prophecy, of reincarnation and of foretelling the future.*